WORKBOOK FOR

THE ELEMENTS OF MUSIC
Concepts and Applications

Volume One   *Second Edition*

RALPH TUREK
The University of Akron

Consulting Editor in Music
ALLAN W. SCHINDLER
Eastman School of Music

McGraw-Hill, Inc.

New York   St. Louis   San Francisco   Auckland   Bogotá   Caracas
Lisbon   London   Madrid   Mexico City   Milan   Montreal
New Delhi   San Juan   Singapore   Sydney   Tokyo   Toronto

WORKBOOK FOR
THE ELEMENTS OF MUSIC
Concepts and Applications
Volume One

5 6 7 8 9 QPD QPD 9 0 9 8

ISBN 0-07-065493-X

This book was set in Baskerville by Music-Book Associates.
The editors were Cynthia Ward and John M. Morriss;
the designer was Carol A. Couch;
the cover was designed by Rafael Hernandez;
cover painting by Jack Ox;
the production supervisor was Kathryn Porzio.
Project supervision was done by The Total Book.
Quebecor Printing/Dubuque was printer and binder.

Contents

Preface

This Workbook is intended to supplement the practice material and assignments found in Volume One of *The Elements of Music: Concepts and Applications.* Each chapter in the Workbook corresponds to a chapter in the text, and has the same title. Like the exercises in the text, the Workbook exercises are of three basic types:

1. analytical and part-writing drills that focus on theoretical problems in isolation, divorced, as it were, from their musical context
2. analytical problems dealing with larger excerpts from the musical literature
3. exercises involving the application of theoretical concepts through actual composition

Also like those in the text, the Workbook exercises are grouped to correspond to the sections *within* the chapters. It is, therefore, not necessary to cover a chapter in its entirety before reinforcing the ideas presented through classroom drill or assignments.

At the same time, the Workbook exercises have been designed to *complement* those of the text by offering subtly different approaches to the theoretical problems. In most cases, space is provided within the Workbook for the answers. The pages are perforated, so that they can be torn out and handed in. Between the exercises of the text and those contained in the Workbook, instructors should have ample material from which to choose for in-class and out-of-class drill or assignments—indeed, it is likely that few if any instructors will feel it necessary to use *all* of the drill material—and students should benefit from the many approaches to any given theoretical problem.

Ralph Turek

Fundamentals

Chapter 1
Pitch and its Notation

PAGES 3–8

A. Before each note, draw the clef (treble, bass, alto, or tenor) that would place the note within the octave designated (see text p. 6 for octave designations). On the line beneath the note, give its letter name and octave designation.

NOTE: There is only one correct answer in each case.

Example:

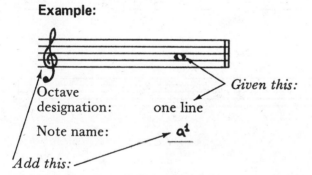

Octave designation: one line

Note name:

Add this:

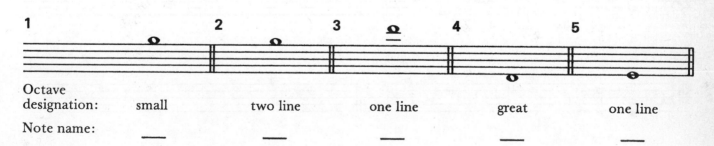

	1	**2**	**3**	**4**	**5**
Octave designation:	small	two line	one line	great	one line
Note name:	—	—	—	—	—

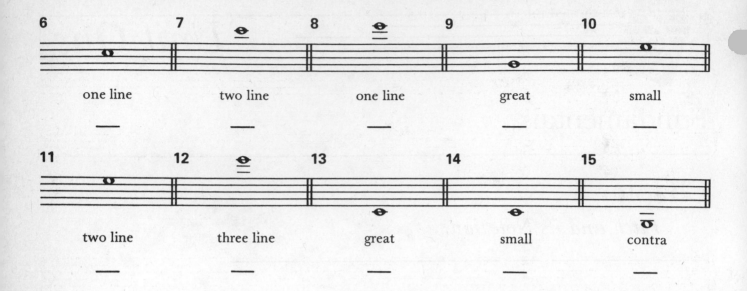

one line   two line   one line   great   small

—   —   —   —   —

two line   three line   great   small   contra

—   —   —   —   —

B. Renotate the following melodic phrases in the clef (treble, alto, tenor, or bass) requiring the fewest notes with ledger lines. If the given clef requires no greater number of notes with ledger lines than any of the other three possibilities, indicate this by writing *O.K.* in the space provided.

C. Provide the indicated pitches in the correct octaves on the grand staff below.

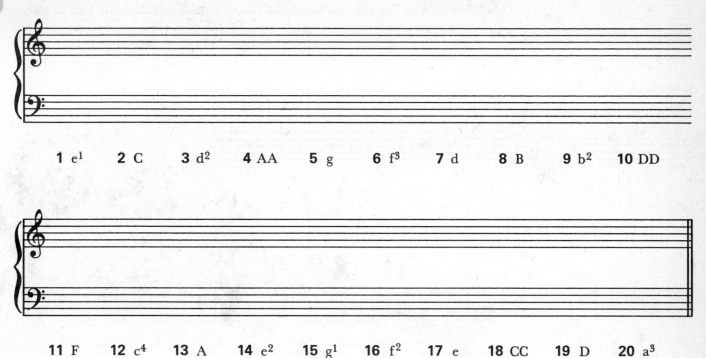

1 e¹   **2** C   **3** d²   **4** AA   **5** g   **6** f³   **7** d   **8** B   **9** b²   **10** DD

11 F   **12** c⁴   **13** A   **14** e²   **15** g¹   **16** f²   **17** e   **18** CC   **19** D   **20** a³

D. Provide the indicated pitches in the correct octaves in alto or tenor clef, as specified.

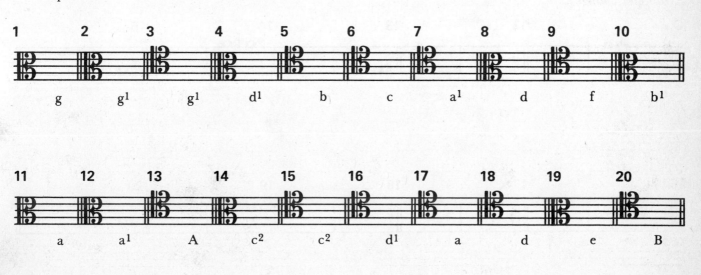

A. Without altering the sounding pitches, rewrite each diatonic half step as a chromatic half step and vice versa. You may respell either one of the pitches, but *not both*. Avoid using double flats or double sharps.

Examples:

Given: *Rewrite as:*   *Given:*   *Rewrite as:*   *(or)*

1   2   3   4   5

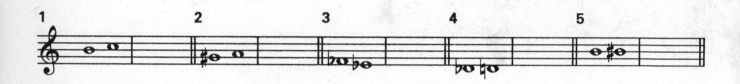

6   7   8   9   10

(Note clef change)

11   12   13   14   15

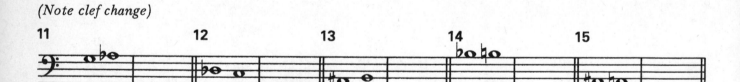

16   17   18   19   20

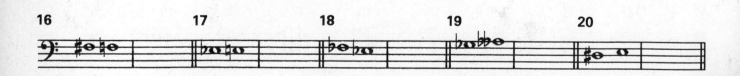

B. Observing the clef sign, notate the specified pitch (in the correct octave). Then construct the specified interval above or below the pitch.

1 Write the given note, then construct a diatonic half step above.

b   g   d¹   G#   a³

2 Write the given note, then construct a chromatic half step below.

c²   e³   a#   BB   f#¹

3 Write the given note, then construct a whole step above, using a pitch with an adjacent letter name.

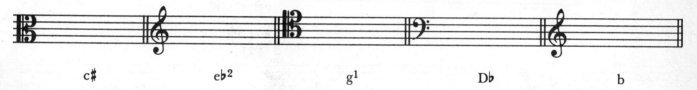

c#   eb²   g¹   Db   b

4 Write the given note, then construct a whole step below, using a pitch with an adjacent letter name.

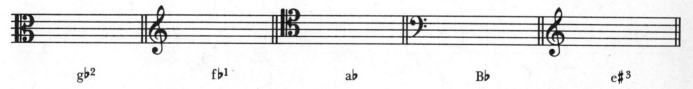

gb²   fb¹   ab   Bb   e#³

C. Using accidentals, alter the *second* pitch in each measure to create a whole step or a half step as specified. Where it is necessary to *cancel* the accidental preceding the second pitch, place the natural sign directly above the staff.

NOTE: In some cases, no alteration is needed. Indicate this by the notation *O.K.*

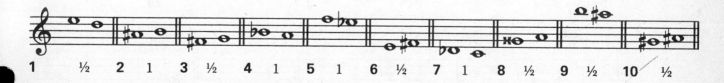

1   ½   2   1   3   ½   4   1   5   1   6   ½   7   1   8   ½   9   ½   10   ½

5

D. Match the enharmonic pitches.

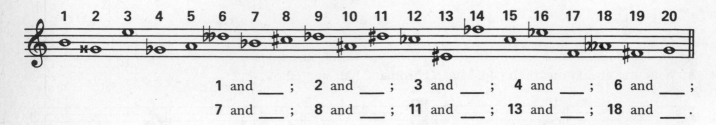

1 and ___ ;   **2** and ___ ;   **3** and ___ ;   **4** and ___ ;   **6** and ___ ;

7 and ___ ;   **8** and ___ ;   **11** and ___ ;   **13** and ___ ;   **18** and ___ .

E. Renotate each of the following intervals enharmonically in two ways. For the first spelling, use the *same* letter name for both pitches. For the second spelling, use *adjacent* letter names. *Do not* use double flats or double sharps.

F. Rewrite the following melodic fragments, respelling enharmonically any
   pitches with accidentals used incorrectly. (Refer to page 11 in the text for
   the proper use of flats and sharps.)

1

2

3

Chapter 2
Rhythm and Other Aspects of Notation

PART ONE

A. Show the single note value equal in duration to the following combined values.

Example:

♩ ♫ = _♩._

1 ♩ ♩ ♬ = ____

2 ♩. ♪ ♩ = _____

3 ♬♬ ♫ = ____

4 ♩ 𝅝 ♬♪ = ____

5 ♬ = _____

6 ♫♩ ♪ ♩.♫ = ____

7 ♪ ♩. 𝅝 = _____

8 ♫♪ ♫ = _____

9 𝅝 ♩ ♪ = _____

10 ♩ ♬ = _____

8

B. Indicate the precise value (the number of beats and fractional parts) spanned by each of the note values *in the indicated meter.*

Examples:

$\frac{12}{8}$ 𝅗𝅥. 𝅗𝅥 2⅔

$\frac{4}{4}$ ♩. ¾

1 $\frac{4}{4}$ 𝅗𝅥.. _____

2 $\frac{4}{2}$ 𝅗𝅥 𝅗𝅥. _____

3 $\frac{9}{8}$ 𝅗𝅥. ♩ _____

4 $\frac{3}{4}$ 𝅗𝅥. ♩ _____

5 $\frac{6}{2}$ 𝅝. 𝅗𝅥. _____
  (𝅝· = beat)

6 $\frac{6}{8}$ 𝅗𝅥. ♪ _____
  (♩· = beat)

7 $\frac{5}{4}$ 𝅗𝅥. 𝅗𝅥.. _____

8 $\frac{4}{16}$ ♩ ♪. _____
  (♪ = beat)

9 $\frac{3}{2}$ 𝅝. 𝅗𝅥. _____

10 $\frac{6}{4}$ 𝅗𝅥. 𝅗𝅥 ♪ _____

C. 1. Identify with T, A, or T-A the tonal and agogic accents in the following melodies.
  2. Decide on the grouping of beats according to these accents and place bar lines at the appropriate points.
  3. Add an appropriate meter signature.

NOTE: The passages may or may not begin on the first beat of a measure.

9

2

3

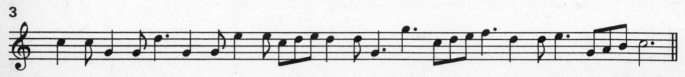

4

D. Give the meter signatures requested and illustrate a single-measure rhythmic pattern that incorporates at least four different types of notes and/or rests.

Example:

Simple triple; 𝅗𝅥 = beat

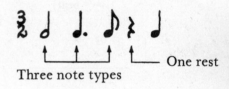

Three note types — One rest

1 Compound quadruple; 𝅗𝅥. = beat _____

2 Simple triple; ♪ = beat _____

3 Simple duple; 𝅗𝅥 = beat _____

4 Compound triple; ♪. = beat _____

5 Simple quadruple; ♪ = beat _____

6 Compound duple; ♩. = beat _____

7 Simple quadruple; ♩ = beat _____

8 Compound duple; 𝅗𝅥. = beat _____

E. Add bar lines to the following rhythmic passages. After adding bar lines,
   rewrite each passage in the meter indicated.

1

Rewrite in $\frac{6}{4}$:

2

Rewrite in $\frac{5}{8}$:

3

Rewrite in $\frac{3}{4}$:

4

Rewrite in $\frac{4}{2}$:

5

Rewrite in $\frac{9}{4}$:

F. Rewrite the following passages so that they sound the same in the new meter. To do so will require the use of borrowed divisions in the new meter.

PARTS TWO and THREE

A. Complete each measure by adding a single note value.

B. From the given list of meters, select the one that is most clearly reflected in each of the two-measure passages that follow. Each of the meters occurs at least once.

Meters: $\frac{3}{8}$ $\frac{5}{8}$ $\frac{6}{8}$ $\frac{9}{8}$ $\frac{3}{4}$ $\frac{6}{4}$ $\frac{3}{2}$ $\frac{4}{2}$

1 ___

2 ___

3 ___

4 ___

5 ___

6 ___

7 ___

8 ___

9 ___

10 ___

C. Renotate each of the following two-measure passages to reflect the meter more clearly and to represent the correct use of beams, dots, ties, and rests.

14

D. Rewrite the following rhythmic passages in the indicated meters so that they sound the same. Rebar, rebeam, and change tied note values or dotted notes so as to produce the most appropriate notation in the new meter. Add rests where necessary to complete the final measure. In most cases, the renotated version will contain more or fewer measures than the original.

5

E. Following are some melodies from the literature. Add the bar lines. Assume that all begin with the first beat of the measure, unless otherwise indicated.

1 Mozart: *String Quartet, K. 421* (IV)

2 Beethoven: *Piano Sonata, Op. 81a* (I)

3 Tartini: *Sonata for Violin and Continuo* (I)

4 Schubert: "Der Müller und der Bach," No. 19 (from *Die schöne Müllerin, D. 795*)

F. Rewrite the following melodies in both the clef and meter indicated. In some cases, you may have to use a borrowed division of the beat in order to duplicate the rhythms exactly.

1

Chapter 3
Scales, Keys, and Intervals

PART ONE

A. Construct the major scale in which:

1 A♭ is the second degree

2 C is the fourth degree

3 E is the fourth degree

4 G is the sixth degree

5 D♯ is the seventh degree

6 C♯ is the eighth degree

7 B♭ is the fifth degree

8 D is the seventh degree

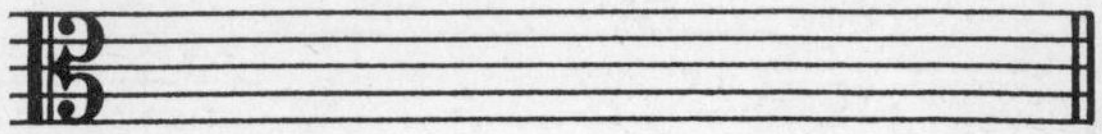

9 F♯ is the third degree

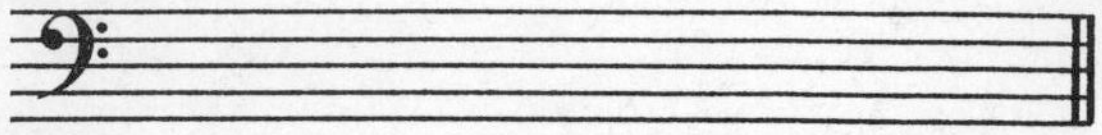

10 B is the fifth degree

B. Write the key signature for the following keys in the clefs indicated. Be sure to draw the clef sign correctly.

1 D♭: tenor clef

2 E♭: alto clef

3 A: treble clef

4 G♭: tenor clef

5 E: bass clef

6 f♯: alto clef

7 c♯: treble clef

8 d♯: bass clef

9 b: tenor clef

10 f: treble clef

C. After each melodic fragment, name and notate the scale upon which it is based.

1 Beethoven: *Piano Sonata, Op. 10, No. 1* (III)

Scale: _____   Scale name: _____

*Disregard this melodic ornament.

2 J. S. Bach: *Sonata for Flute and Continuo, BWV 1034* (I)

Scale: _____   Scale name: _____

3 Mozart: *Die Entführung aus dem Serail, K. 384* (Act II, No. 8)

Scale:

Scale name: _____

4 Schumann: *Symphonic Etudes, Op. 13* (Theme)

Scale:

Scale name: _____

D. Construct the following scales, in treble clef, placing all necessary flats or sharps before the pitches.

1 The relative minor (melodic) of A major

2 The relative major of B♭ minor

3 The relative minor (harmonic) of G♭ major

4 The parallel minor (natural) of A♭ major

5 The parallel major of E minor

6 The relative minor (harmonic) of F major

7 The parallel major of C♯ minor

8 The relative major of G minor

Unscramble the pitch collections below in order to form a major, harmonic minor, or melodic minor scale. In each case, only one possible scale can be formed from the pitch material. Some pitches may have to be transposed by an octave in order to complete the scale within a single octave.

24

F. The following melodies are based on the natural minor scale. Add the accidentals you would expect to find if the melodies were instead based on the melodic minor scale. Remember that the sixth and seventh degrees normally are raised when their goal is the tonic and are in their natural minor form when their goal is the dominant.

NOTE: Be careful to observe the clef.

PART TWO

A. Notate the requested pitches in the indicated clefs.

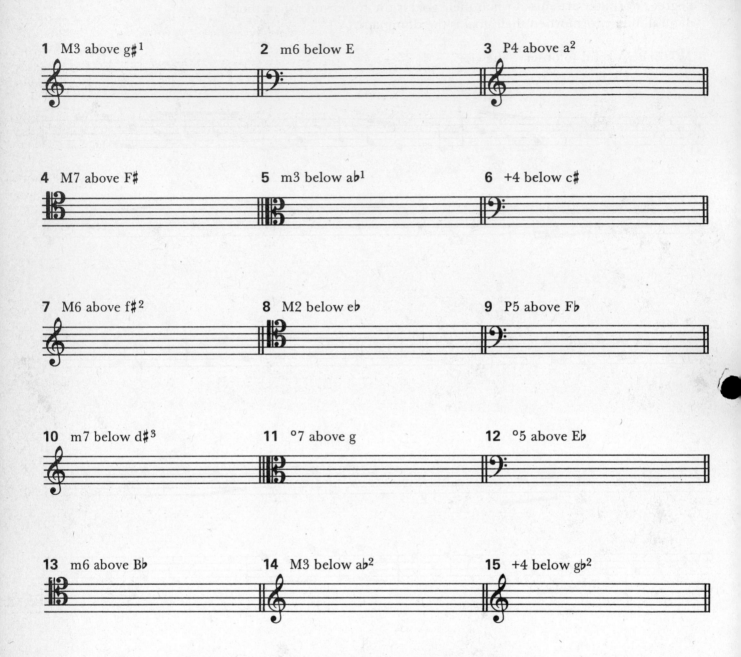

1 M3 above g♯¹

2 m6 below E

3 P4 above a²

4 M7 above F♯

5 m3 below a♭¹

6 +4 below c♯

7 M6 above f♯²

8 M2 below e♭

9 P5 above F♭

10 m7 below d♯³

11 °7 above g

12 °5 above E♭

13 m6 above B♭

14 M3 below a♭²

15 +4 below g♭²

B. 1. Identify the intervals in each measure.
   2. Name the major or minor scale containing the fewest number of flats
      or sharps in which all three notes appear.
   3. Indicate the scale degree each note represents.
   4. For minor scales, indicate whether the form is melodic or harmonic.

Example 1:

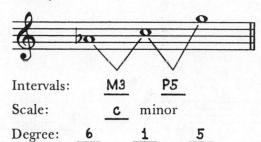

Intervals: M3   P5

Scale: c   minor

Degree: 6   1   5

Melodic or harmonic: harmonic

Example 2:

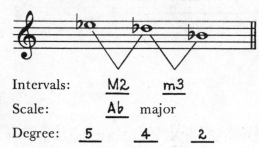

Intervals: M2   m3

Scale: Ab   major

Degree: 5   4   2

NOTE: Although Db, Gb, and Cb are also major scales containing these
three pitches, Ab is the one containing the *fewest* flats and is therefore the
preferred answer.

1   2   3

Intervals: __   __   __   __   __

Scale: __ minor   __ minor   __ major

Degree: __   __   __   __   __   __   __

Melodic or harmonic: _____   _____

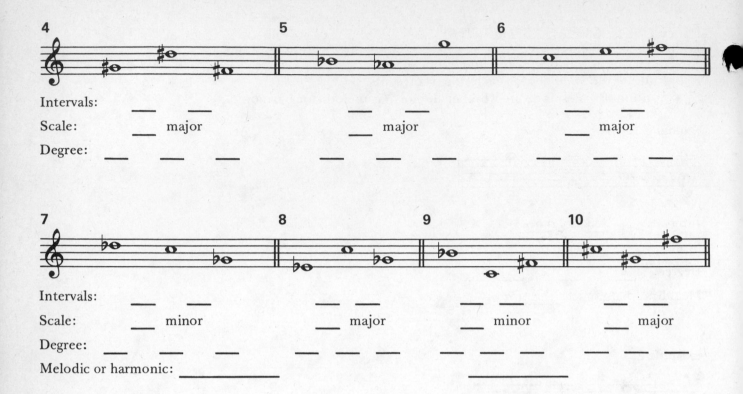

Intervals: ___   ___   ___   ___   ___   ___

Scale: ___ major   ___ major   ___ major

Degree: ___   ___   ___   ___   ___   ___   ___   ___   ___

Intervals: ___   ___   ___   ___   ___   ___   ___   ___

Scale: ___ minor   ___ major   ___ minor   ___ major

Degree: ___   ___   ___   ___   ___   ___   ___   ___   ___   ___   ___   ___

Melodic or harmonic: _____   _____

C. Spell each of the following intervals enharmonically so that the numerical value and quality of the interval remain the same. Identify the interval. The first answer is provided for you.

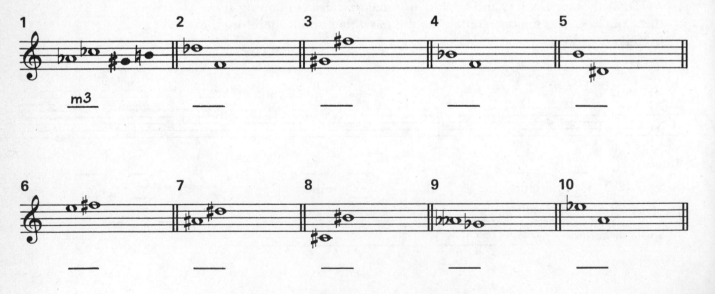

D. Identify the following intervals. Then, respell the *second* note in each
interval enharmonically so that the sound remains the same but the
numerical value and quality are different. Identify the new interval.

Example:

Given:

m7   +6

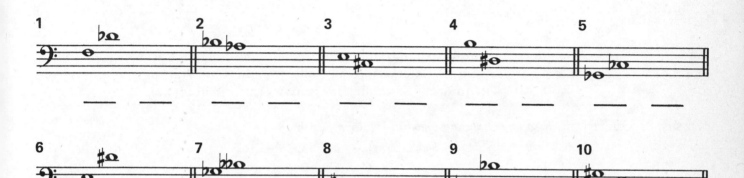

1   2   3   4   5

6   7   8   9   10

E. Expand the simple intervals to compound intervals, and vice versa. Be
sure to observe the indicated clefs.

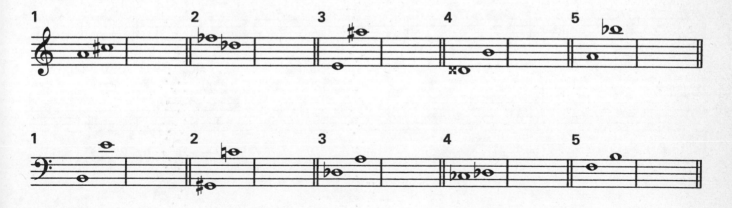

1   2   3   4   5

1   2   3   4   5

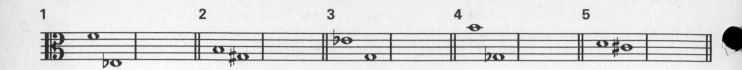

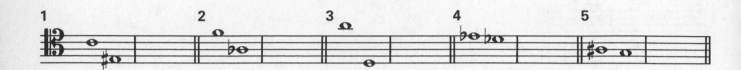

F. Identify each harmonic interval in the following musical passage. In classifying the intervals, reduce all compound intervals to simple intervals. The intervals of the first measure are identified for you.

Lassus: "Credo" from *Missa ad imitationem moduli Doulce memoire*

NOTE: The symbol 𝄞 indicates that the part is to sound an octave lower.

Unit Two

The Basic Harmonic Vocabulary:
The Structure and Use of Chords

Chapter 4

*Harmony I: Introduction to Triads and
Seventh Chords; Inversion; Chord Symbols
and Figured Bass*

PART ONE

A. Next to each of the following chords, make the *single alteration* that will
   create the requested type of triad.

Example:

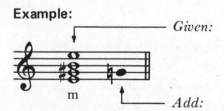

 1   2   3   4   5

        +   M   m   °   m

 6   7   8   9   10

        +   M   °   °   m

                                                                         31

B. Construct the specified triads. The letter name symbols indicate both the root and triad quality.

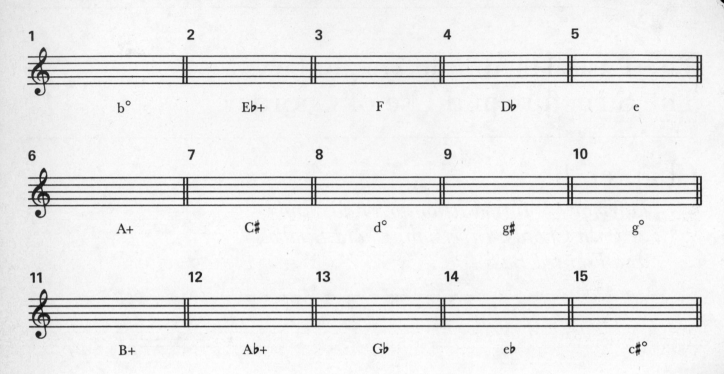

1	2	3	4	5
b°	E♭+	F	D♭	e

6	7	8	9	10
A+	C♯	d°	g♯	g°

11	12	13	14	15
B+	A♭+	G♭	e♭	c♯°

C. Beneath each triad, write the letter name symbol that reflects the root and triad quality.

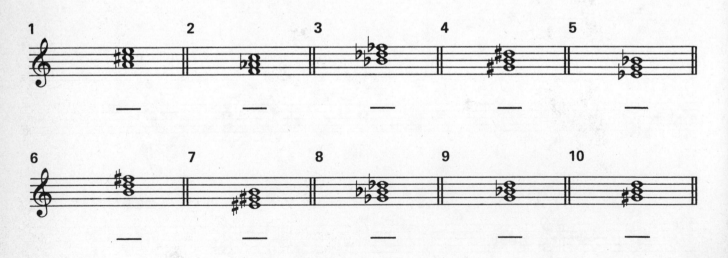

32

D. Given M, m, +, or °, treat each pitch first as the root, then as the third, and finally as the fifth of the triad. Construct the specified triad types.

Example:

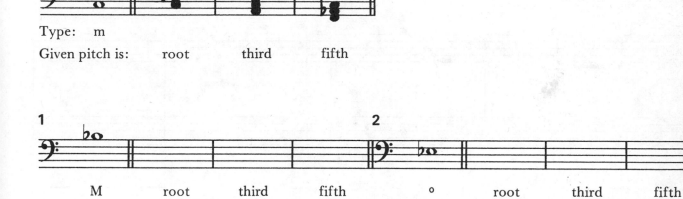

Type:　　m
Given pitch is:　　root　　third　　fifth

1

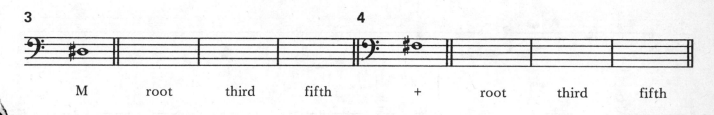

M　　root　　third　　fifth　　　°　　root　　third　　fifth

3

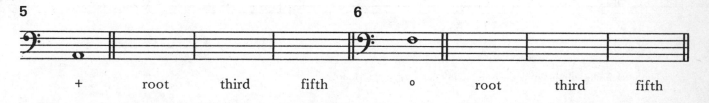

M　　root　　third　　fifth　　　+　　root　　third　　fifth

5

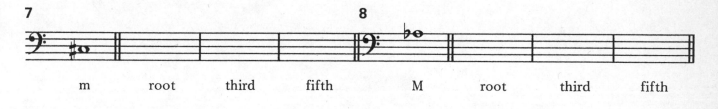

+　　root　　third　　fifth　　　°　　root　　third　　fifth

7

m　　root　　third　　fifth　　　M　　root　　third　　fifth

9

M　　root　　third　　fifth　　　m　　root　　third　　fifth

E. Give the letter name for each *complete* triad (those containing a root, third, and fifth) in the following excerpt. Use an upper- or lower-case letter, with a + or ° as necessary, to show the triad's quality. Place an X below each chord that is *not* a complete triad.

1 Haydn: *Piano Sonata No. 17* (Menuetto)*

*This work is of doubtful authenticity. It has not been assigned a Hoboken number.

A. Indicate the inversion (R = root position, 1 = first inversion, 2 = second inversion) and quality (using M, m, +, or °) of the following triads.

Example:

Inversion: __2__

Quality: __M__

| 1 | 2 | 3 | 4 | 5 | 6 | 7 | 8 | 9 | 10 |

Inversion: ___ ___ ___ ___ ___ ___ ___ ___ ___ ___

Quality: ___ ___ ___ ___ ___ ___ ___ ___ ___ ___

B. Stack the chords in their simplest position, maintaining the lowest sounding pitch. Then, in the first blank, indicate by letter name symbol, the
   chord root, and the quality of the triad. In the second blank, indicate the
   inversion (R, 1, or 2).

Examples:

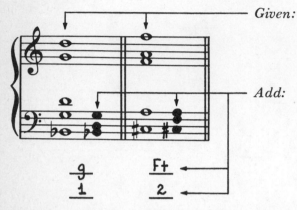

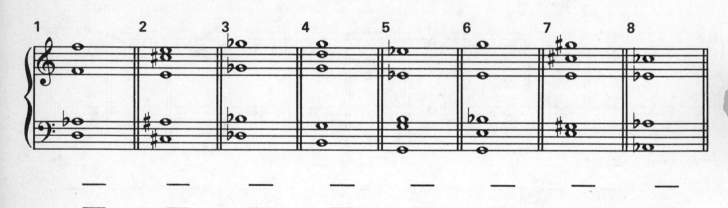

C. Construct three triads of the same type, as specified, that employ the given
pitch as a chord member. Retain the given pitch as the lowest sounding
member of the triad. The first triad should be in root position, the second
in first inversion, and the third in second inversion, as indicated.

Example:

m: R   1   2

PART THREE

A. Construct the triads indicated by the figured bass symbols.

37

B. Add the pitches necessary to form complete triads above each bass note. Then place the correct letter name symbols (showing root, quality, and inversion) in the blanks beneath the notes.

C. Beneath the bass line, add the figured bass symbols that would accurately represent each passage.

1 J. S. Bach: "O du Liebe meiner Liebe" (adaptation)

2 J. S. Bach: "Nur mein Jesus ist mein Leben"

D. In the blanks beneath each chord, provide the appropriate letter name symbol. Add appropriate superscripts to indicate inversions. Disregard all circled tones. Place an *X* in the blank beneath each incomplete triad.

1 Bourgeois: *Doxology*

G: __ __ __ __ __ __ __ __ __ __ __ __ __ __ __ __

2 Cruger: "Herr, ich habe missgehandelt"

Chapter 5
Harmony II: Diatonic Triads in Major and Minor Keys; Functional Tonal Principles

PART ONE:

A. Add the key signature and then illustrate the indicated triads in root position. Be sure to observe the clef signs.

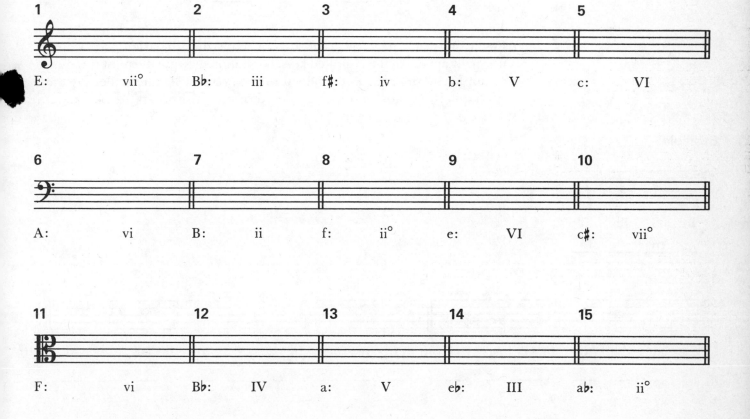

1. E: vii°
2. B♭: iii
3. f♯: iv
4. b: V
5. c: VI

6. A: vi
7. B: ii
8. f: ii°
9. e: VI
10. c♯: vii°

11. F: vi
12. B♭: IV
13. a: V
14. e♭: III
15. a♭: ii°

B. Beneath each triad, write the Roman numerals that reflect its functions in the indicated keys.

1		2		3		4		5	
D:	___	Db:	___	ab:	___	d#:	___	Ab:	___
E:	___	bb:	___	Cb:	___	F#:	___	c:	___
f#:	___	c:	___			E:	___	g:	___

6		7		8		9		10	
A:	___	F#:	___	eb:	___	Eb:	___	A:	___
D:	___	d#:	___	Cb:	___	d:	___	f#:	___
f#:	___			Db:	___	F:	___		

C. Regarding each pitch as a chord root, construct the triad as it would normally appear in the indicated keys. For minor keys, use the most common minor-key harmonies, as explained on text page 124. Then, identify the triad quality (major, minor, augmented or diminished) in the blank.

Example:

In: G   Bb   f#
    m   o   M

1			2			3			4			5		
In: d	Eb	c	In: Gb	g	eb	In: c#	B	A	In: e	F	b	In: Db	Cb	Ab
___			___			___			___			___		

6			7			8			9			10		
In: B	f#	E	In: Ab	f	bb	In: Bb	C	Ab	In: b	g#	F#	In: eb	Cb	Db
___			___			___			___			___		

42

D. Add the appropriate key signature and show the bass note and figured
   bass symbol that represent each of the following chords.

Example:

First-inversion
supertonic

Key: Bb   **6**

1 Second-inversion tonic	**2** First-inversion mediant	**3** Root-position submediant	**4** Second-inversion subdominant	**5** Second-inversion supertonic

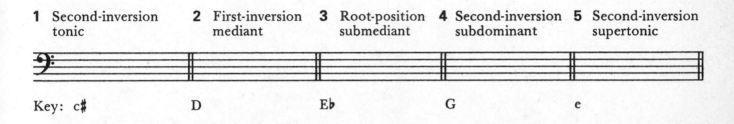

Key: c#   D   Eb   G   e

6 Root-position dominant	**7** First-inversion leading tone	**8** First-inversion submediant	**9** Second-inversion tonic	**10** First-inversion leading tone

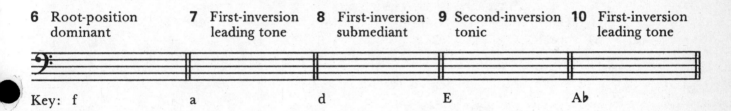

Key: f   a   d   E   Ab

PART TWO

A. Write the chords that represent the indicated harmonic motions in the
   given keys. Then, identify the type of harmonic motion as a progression
   (P), retrogression (R), or repetition (S, for same function).

1 f: ii°   V   **2** A: V   vi   **3** Eb: iii   vi   **4** G: ii   IV   **5** B: iii   IV

_____   _____   _____   _____   _____

6 eb: VI   iv   **7** D: V   I   **8** g: VI   III   **9** F: IV   vi   **10** E: vi   ii

_____   _____   _____   _____   _____

B. Circle the tonic in each of the following chord successions. (There will be only one key in which all of the chords are diatonic.) Then, using the letters P (progression), R (retrogression) and S (same function), indicate the type of harmonic motion between the chords. Use an X to signify motion *from* the tonic triad.

Example:

E - Ⓐ - D - E - f#
<u>P</u>   <u>X</u>   <u>P</u>   <u>R</u>

1   G♭ - e♭ - c^{ø7} - F - b♭
   ___ ___ ___ ___

2   d - g - d - A - B♭
   ___ ___ ___ ___

3   C - a - D - e - C - D - G
   ___ ___ ___ ___ ___ ___

4   F - d - g - C - a - d - C
   ___ ___ ___ ___ ___ ___

5   E♭ - A♭ - f - B♭ - g - c - B♭
   ___ ___ ___ ___ ___ ___

6   F# - b - G - a#° - b - e - F#
   ___ ___ ___ ___ ___ ___

7   E - g# - A - B - E - A - B
   ___ ___ ___ ___ ___ ___

8   C - D♭ - b♭ - g° - f - C - f
   ___ ___ ___ ___ ___ ___

9   c - b° - c - f - A♭ - G - c
   ___ ___ ___ ___ ___ ___

10   g# - E - c# - a#° - F# - B - F#
   ___ ___ ___ ___ ___ ___

C. Indicate the key(s) in which each of the following chords functions as a dominant seventh or supertonic seventh chord.

44

D. Provide harmonic analysis of the following excerpt. Disregard circled tones, which are not members of the harmonies. Then identify the motion between the harmonies in this manner: P = progression; R = retrogression; S = same function. Use an X to signify motion *from* the tonic triad.

Schubert: *Originaltanz, Op. 9, No. 3**

Key ___ : _____ _____ _____

Harmonic motion: ___ ___ ___ ___ ___ ___

___ ___ ___ ___

___ ___ ___ ___ ___ ___

*This piece is contained in its entirety in *Analytical Anthology of Music,* second edition, by Ralph Turek (McGraw-Hill, Inc., 1992).

Chapter 6
Harmony III: Harmonic Cadences; Embellishing Tones; Principles of Harmonization

PART ONE

A. Name the cadence (authentic, plagal, half, deceptive, or Phrygian half) which:

1 Ends on a G minor triad in the key of B♭: _____

2 Ends on a D major triad in the key of G: _____

3 Involves a root movement from B to F♯ in F♯ minor: _____

4 Involves a descending fifth root movement from G♯ in the key of C♯ minor: _____

5 Involves a descending bass from C to B in E minor: _____

B. Add the key signature and notate a figured bass that would indicate the following cadences.

Examples:

Deceptive: E♭ major

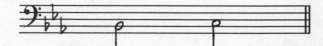

Phrygian half: G minor

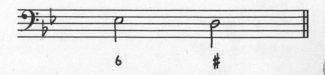

1 Phrygian half: F minor

2 Authentic: C minor

3 Half: B minor

4 Plagal: A♭ major

5 Plagal: E♭ minor

6 Half: E major

7 Authentic: F♯ major

8 Deceptive: D minor

9 Phrygian half: A minor

10 Deceptive: B Major

C. In the following passages:

1. Indicate the key.
2. Provide Roman numeral analysis.
3. Indicate the type of cadence.

Disregard the circled tones.

1 J. S. Bach: "Wer weiss, wie nahe mir mein Ende"

Key ___ : __ __ __ __ __ __ __ __

Cadence: _____

2 Chopin: *Nocturne, Op. 37, No. 1*

Key ___ : __ __ __ __ __ __ __ __ __ __ __ __

Cadence: _____

3 J. S. Bach: "Wer nur den lieben Gott lässt walten"

Key ___ : __ __ __ __ __ __ __ __

Cadence: _____

4 Schumann: *Album for the Young, Op. 68* (No. 8, "Wild Rider")*

Allegro con brio

Key ____ : ___ ___ ___ ___

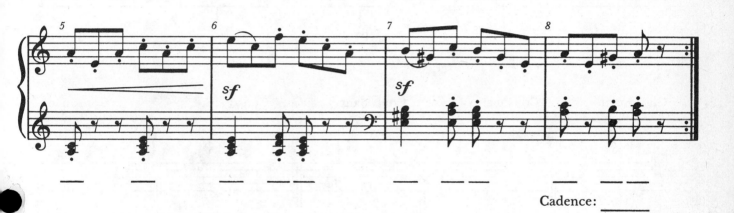

Cadence: _____

*This movement is contained in its entirety in *Anthology for Musical Analysis*, fifth edition, by Charles Burkhart (Harcourt Brace College Publishers, 1994).

5 Corelli: *Concerto Grosso, Op. 6, No. 8* (IV)

Key ____ : ___ ___ ___ ___

Cadence: _____

PART TWO

A. Add the requested nonchord tone at the designated point. For numbers
6–10, also add the appropriate consonant tone at the point indicated.

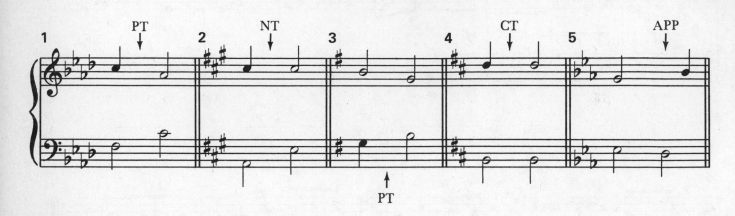

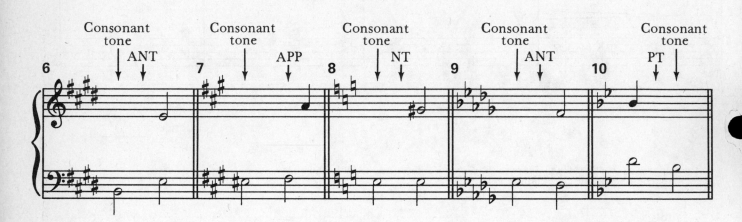

B. Add the specified nonchord tone in the indicated voice. You may have to change some of the given note values to do this.

Example:

4-3 SUS: soprano

1 PT: alto **2** ET: soprano **3** APP: soprano

4 PT: alto **5** PT: tenor **6** APP: soprano

7 ANT: soprano **8** Double PT: tenor and alto **9** NT: tenor **10** 9-8 SUS: tenor

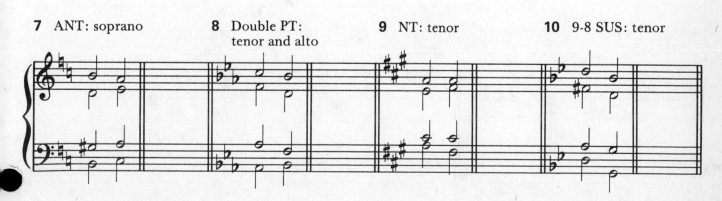

C. At the point indicated, add the specified nonchord tone in a voice that will accommodate it. You may have to change some of the note values to do this.

Example:

ANT:
beat 2

1 ET:
   beat 2

2 9-8 SUS:
   beats 3-4

3 2-3 SUS:
   beats 3-4

4 NT:
   beat 2

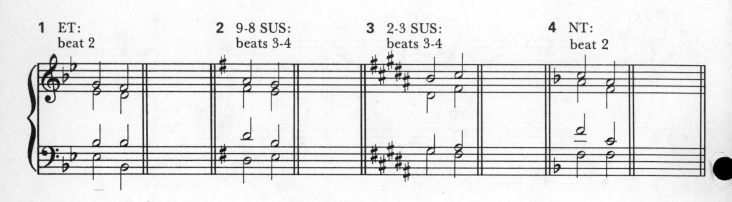

5 PT:
   beat 2

6 ANT:
   beat 2

7 ET:
   beat 2

8 9-10 RET:
   beats 3-4

9 CT:
   beat 2

10 4-3 SUS:
    beats 3-4

D. Following are several phrases from chorale harmonizations by J. S. Bach. Some of the nonchord tones have been removed. Provide a harmonic analysis. Disregard chords marked with an *X*. Then circle and label any nonchord tones that you find.

1 J. S. Bach: "Nun lob', mein Seel', den Herren"

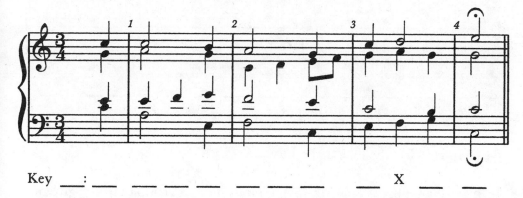

Key ___ : __ __ __ __ __ __ __ X __ __ __

2 J. S. Bach: "Christus, der ist mein Leben"

Key ___ : __ __ __ __ __ __ __ __

3 J. S. Bach: "Auf meinen lieben Gott"

Key ___ : __ __ __ __ __ __ __ __ __ __ __ __ __

4 J. S. Bach: "O Ewigkeit, du Donnerwort"

Key ___ : ___ ___ ___ ___ ___ ___ ___ ___ ___ X

PART THREE

A. In the blank spaces beneath each melody tone or group of tones, give the Roman numeral symbol of the triad(s) in which the tone(s) might be found. Then, choose a succession of harmonies based upon the functional harmonic principles discussed in the chapter and indicate your choice by circling a chord for each melody tone.

B. Using the procedure outlined in Part Three of the chapter, harmonize the following melodies, writing out the chords in root position beneath each appropriate melody tone. Then, create a more pianistic accompaniment, as described on page 165.

NOTE: A new chord need not accompany every melody note.

Part-Writing Triads

Chapter 7

Voice Leading I: Melodic Principles in Four-Part Writing; Voicing Chords; Principles of Chord Connection; Connecting Root-Position Triads

PART ONE

A. In the following chorale harmonizations:

1. Show the range of each voice part.
2. For each voice, indicate the number of times leaps larger than a third occur.
3. Indicate which voice contains the *largest* leaps.
4. Identify the most disjunct voice overall.

1 J. S. Bach: "Du Friedensfürst, Herr Jesu Christ"

Range:

S   A   T   B

Number of leaps
larger than a third: _____ _____ _____ _____

Voice containing the largest leaps: _____

Most disjunct voice: _____

2 J. S. Bach: "Ach Gott, wie manches Herzelied"

Range:

Number of leaps
larger than a third: _____ _____ _____ _____

Voice containing the largest leaps: _____

Most disjunct voice: _____

B. Play and sing the following melodies. Then identify those features *not* in
keeping with the melodic principles of the chorale style.

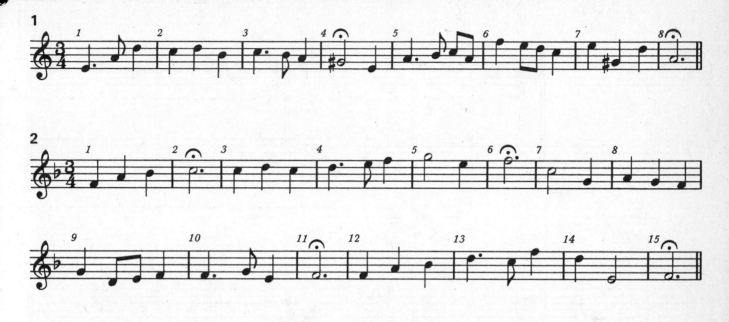

PART TWO

A. Indicate the type (major, minor, diminished, or augmented), structure
(O for open, C for close), and inversion of each triad.

Type: — — — — — — — — — —
Structure: — — — — — — — — — —
Inversion: — — — — — — — — — —

B. Revoice all close structures as open structures and vice versa, retaining the same soprano and bass pitches. Then, identify both structures (O for open, C for close).

C. Place an *X* above those chords which are *not* doubled according to the most common doubling procedures outlined on pages 187–188 of the text. Be sure to take the key into consideration.

Key: e   a   Ab   F   g   E   Bb   Eb   c   b

D. In the following chorale harmonization:

1. Indicate with Roman numerals and superscripts the function and inversion of each chord.
2. Above any root-position triad in which the root is not doubled, write a *3* or *5* to indicate the doubled chord member. Write *INC* above any incomplete triads.

Disregard chords enclosed in boxes and be sure to be aware of the indicated key changes.

Schop: "Werde munter mein Gemüte"

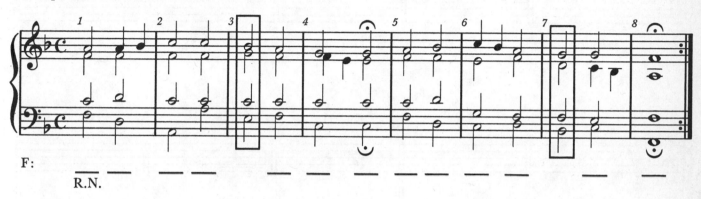

F:

R.N.

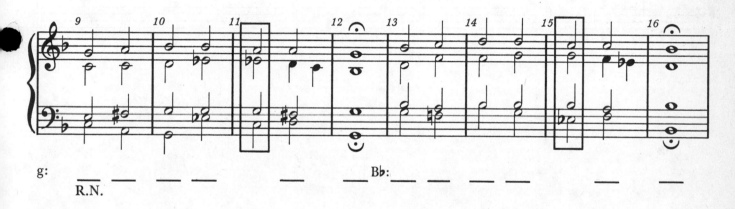

g:

R.N.

Bb:

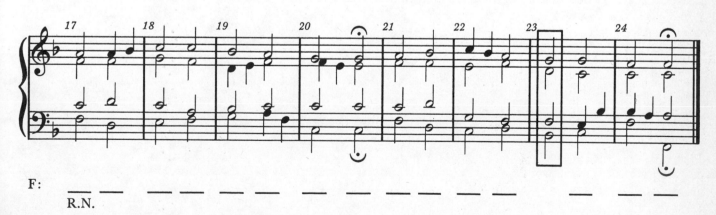

F:

R.N.

E. Write the indicated chords for four voices in the specified structure, doubling the root. In each case, add the required key signature (and accidentals, if necessary).

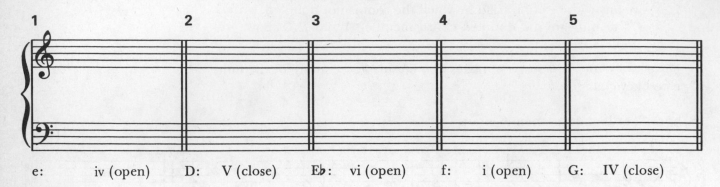

e: iv (open)   D: V (close)   E♭:   vi (open)   f: i (open)   G: IV (close)

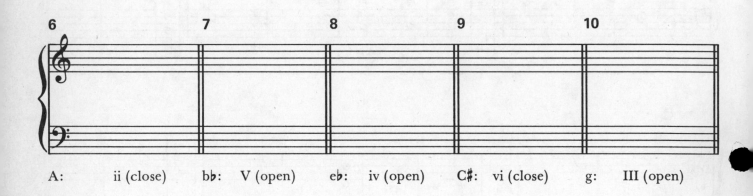

A: ii (close)   b♭:   V (open)   e♭:   iv (open)   C♯:   vi (close)   g: III (open)

A. Identify the type of motion (*C* = contrary; *O* = oblique; *S* = similar; *P* = parallel) between the soprano and bass in the following chorale fragments. Where one pitch is sustained while another changes, regard the sustained pitch as a repeated note. (A blank is not provided where *both* soprano and bass remain on the same pitch or an octave transposition of a pitch.)

J. S. Bach, "Ach, dass nicht die letzte Stunde"

J. S. Bach: "Brunnquell aller Güter"

B. Above the given bass line, add a soprano voice that exhibits the prescribed motion against the bass. Each harmonic interval formed should be a consonance. Try to achieve a balanced interval structure. Be careful to avoid consecutive fifths, octaves, or unisons. (*C* = contrary; *O* = oblique; *S* = similar; *P* = parallel.)

C. Identify the voice-leading errors in the following three-chord successions. (More than one error may appear in a single example.) Provide harmonic analysis.

Key ___ : ___ ___ ___   Key ___ : ___ ___ ___   Key ___ : ___ ___ ___

Key ___ : ___ ___ ___   Key ___ : ___ ___ ___   Key ___ : ___ ___ ___   Key ___ : ___ ___ ___

Key ___ : ___ ___ ___   Key ___ : ___ ___ ___   Key ___ : ___ ___ ___

PART FOUR

A. Part-write in four voices the following two-chord successions, using
appropriate doubling, spacing, and chord connection procedures.

1 Root-position chords in fifth relationship

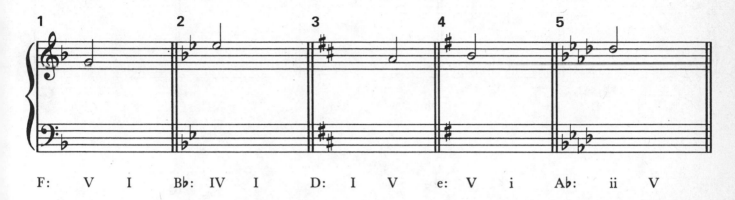

F: V I   Bb: IV I   D: I V   e: V i   Ab: ii V

f#: iv i   Eb: vi ii   C: iii vi   d: V i   Gb: IV I

2 Root-position chords in second and third relationship

f#:   i   III   Bb: IV   V   Db: V   vi   b: i   VI   B: V   vi

d: VI   iv   c: III   v   G: IV   V   g: i   VI   E: V   vi

B. Add the key signature and illustrate in four voices the following cadences,
using the specified structure and the appropriate voice-leading practices.
Provide harmonic analysis.

1 Plagal: open structure

g: _____ _____

2 Authentic: close structure

c#: _____ _____ _____

3 Half: open structure

E: _____ _____ _____

4 Deceptive: open structure

Db: _____ _____ _____

5 Phrygian half: open structure

b: _____ _____ _____

6 Plagal: close structure

Ab: _____ _____ _____

C. Add alto and tenor to the given soprano-bass frameworks (all chords are to be in root position). Then provide harmonic analysis.

1

Key ___ : __ __ __ __ __ __ __ __ __

2

Key ___ : __ __ __ __ __ __ __ __ __ __

3

Key ___ : __ __ __ __ __ __ __ __ __ __

Chapter 8
Voice Leading II: Triads in First Inversion; Part Writing Using Nonchord Tones

PART ONE

A. Write for four voices the triad indicated by the figured bass symbols and key signatures, using the structure specified and appropriate doubling.

Example:

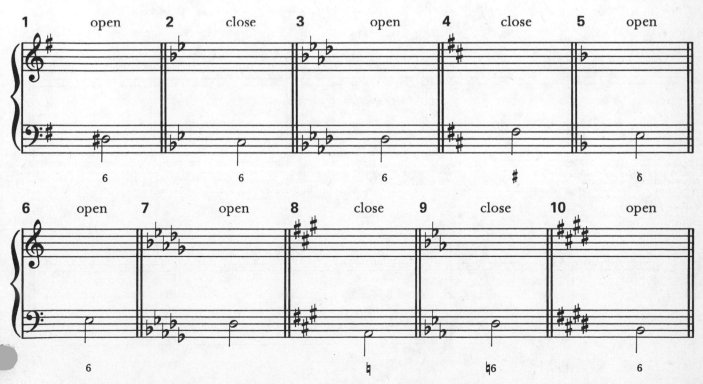

B. Write the indicated chords for four voices in the specified structure, using appropriate doubling. In each case, add the required key signature (and accidentals, if necessary).

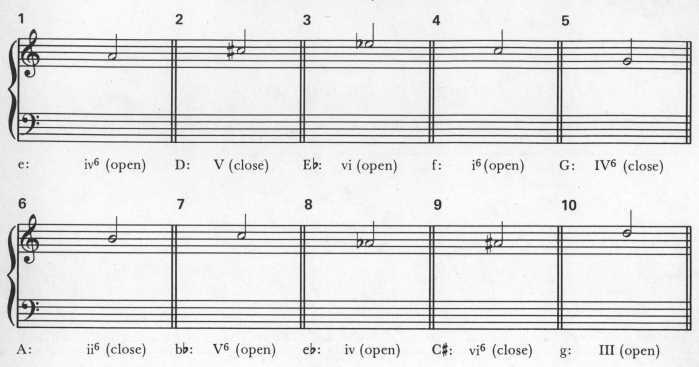

e: iv⁶ (open)   D: V (close)   E♭: vi (open)   f: i⁶ (open)   G: IV⁶ (close)

A: ii⁶ (close)   b♭: V⁶ (open)   e♭: iv (open)   C♯: vi⁶ (close)   g: III (open)

PART TWO

A. Part-write in four voices the following two-chord successions, using appropriate doubling, spacing, and chord connection procedures.

C: I   V⁶   f: iv⁶   V   E♭: IV   I⁶   A: I⁶   IV   e: ii°⁶   V

F: IV⁶   V⁶   B♭: V⁶   vi   E: I   IV⁶   a: V⁶   i   D♭: ii⁶   V

70

B. Complete the following passages in four voices. Then provide harmonic
   analysis where needed.

A: ___ ___ ___   f: ___ ___ ___   d: ___ ___ ___

E: I⁶   IV   V   E♭: ___ ___ ___   C: V⁶   I   I⁶

e: ___   V   i   f♯: ___ ___ ___   b♭: ___ ___ ___

D♭:   I⁶   IV⁶   V

C. Realize the following figured bass lines by adding soprano, alto, and tenor. Observe appropriate voice-leading procedures. Then provide harmonic analysis.

1

Key ___ : ___ ___ ___ ___ ___ ___ ___ ___ ___ ___ ___ ___ ___ ___ ___ ___

2

Key ___ : ___ ___ ___ ___ ___ ___ ___ ___ ___ ___ ___

3

Key ___ : ___ ___ ___ ___ ___ ___ ___ ___ ___ ___ ___

D. **1** Provide harmonic analysis in the blanks beneath the following chorale harmonization. Disregard chords enclosed in boxes, which are either seventh chords or chromatic harmonies not yet discussed.

2 For each of the first-inversion triads present:

a Indicate beneath the chord whether the doubled tone is the soprano (S), the bass (B), or neither (X).

b In how many cases is the soprano the doubled tone? _____ The bass? _____ Neither? _____

c Indicate where common tones have been retained in the same voice from chords preceding or following the first-inversion triad. Do this by connecting common tones with a blue or red line.

3 Would it be accurate to generalize that, where a common tone exists between a first-inversion triad and the preceding and following chords, it is retained in the same voice? _____ (Yes or No)

J. S. Bach: "Du Friedenfürst, Herr Jesu Christ"

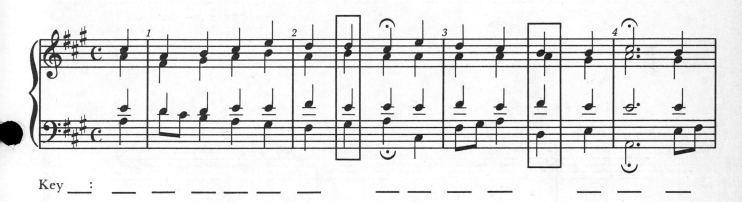

Key ___: ___ ___ ___ ___ ___ ___ ___ ___ ___ ___ ___ ___

___ ___ ___ ___ ___ ___ ___ ___ ___ ___

A. Following is an excerpt from a chorale harmonization by J. S. Bach in which the nonchord tones have been removed. Provide harmonic analysis, disregarding chords enclosed in boxes. Then add nonchord tones as indicated. (This will involve altering existing note values in the affected voice.)

J. S. Bach: "Nun lob', mein Seel', den Herren"

Key ___ : ___ ___ ___ ___ ___ ___ ___ ___

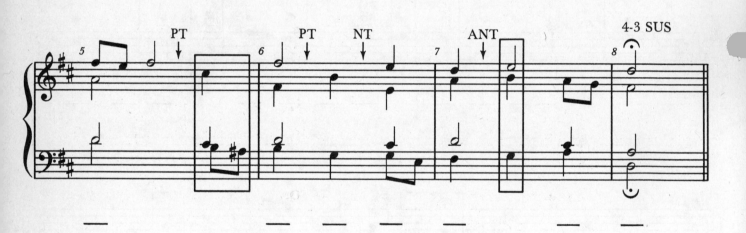

___

B. Part-write the following two-chord successions, using appropriate voice-leading procedures. Remember that the final number in the suspension figure suggests the type of chord (root position, first inversion, or second inversion) that will occur at the point of resolution. (For example, a *6* in the suspension resolution suggests a first-inversion triad.)

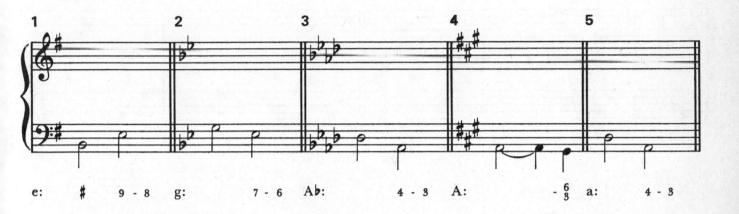

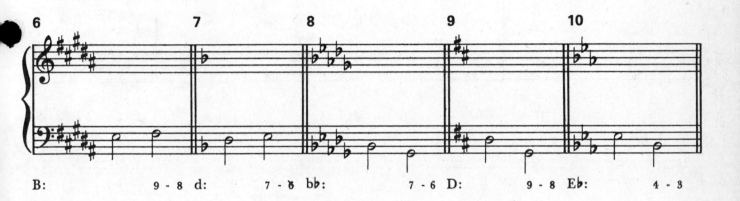

C. Complete the following passages in four voices. As in figured bass notation, single superscripts appearing between chords indicate passing tones. The hyphenated combinations (9-8, 7-6, and 4-3) indicate suspensions.

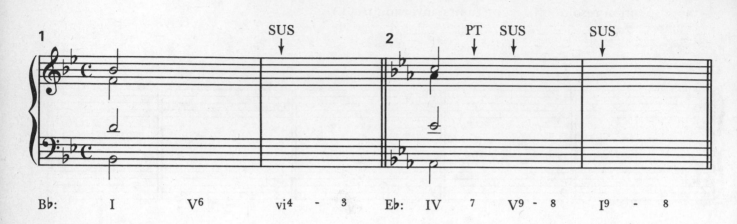

B♭:   I   V⁶   vi⁴ - ³   E♭:   IV   ⁷   V⁹ - ⁸   I⁹ - ⁸

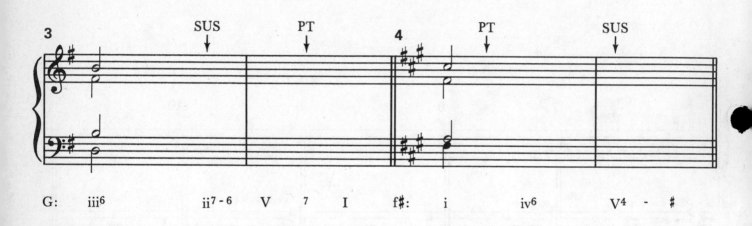

G: iii⁶   ii⁷⁻⁶   V   ⁷   I   f♯:   i   iv⁶   V⁴ - ♯

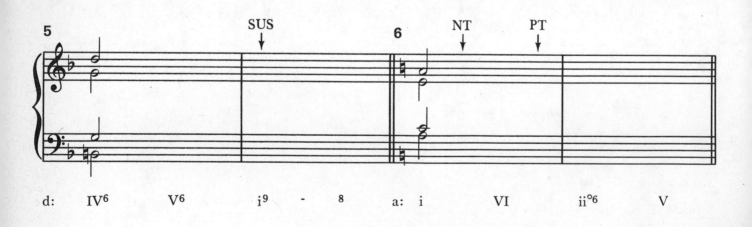

d: IV⁶   V⁶   i⁹ - ⁸   a: i   VI   ii°⁶   V

D. Complete the following passages for four voices and provide harmonic analysis where needed. Add nonchord tones as suggested.

1

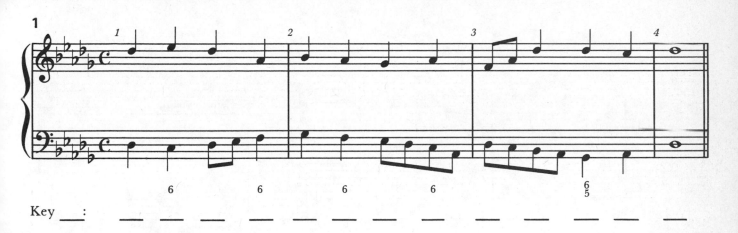

Key ___ : ___ ___ ___ ___ ___ ___ ___ ___ ___ ___ ___

2

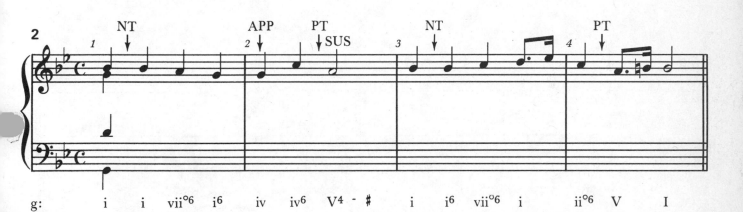

g: i   i   vii°⁶   i⁶   iv   iv⁶   V⁴ - ♯   i   i⁶   vii°⁶   i   ii°⁶   V   I

3

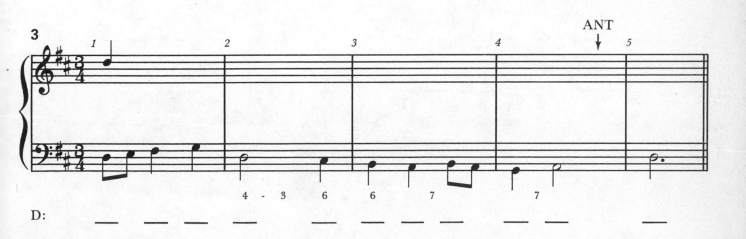

D: ___ ___ ___ ___ ___ ___ ___ ___ ___ ___ ___

E. Provide harmonic analysis of the following chorale harmonizations. Circle and label all nonchord tones. Identify any departures from the part-writing norms that we have discussed and speculate on possible reasons for the departures.

1 J. S. Bach: "Was mein Gott will, das"

Key ___ : _____ , b: _____

2 J. S. Bach: "Was Gott tut, das ist wohlgetan"

Key ___ : _____

*The missing chord third here is supplied by the viola, which doubles the tenor line in the complete orchestration of this chorale, as found in Bach's *Cantata No. 69* ("Lobe den Herrn, meine Seele").

Chapter 9
Voice Leading III: Triads in Second Inversion

PART ONE

A. For the following excerpts:

   1. Provide harmonic analysis.
   2. Identify the types of six-four chords used.

1 Schubert: "Der Müller und der Bach" (from *Die schöne Müllerin, D. 795*)

Key ___: ___ ___ ___ ___ ___ ___ ___ ___

2 Beethoven: *Piano Sonata, Op. 2, No. 3* (III)

Key ___: ___ ___ ___ ___ ___ ___ ___ ___

3 Beethoven: *Piano Sonata, Op. 26* (III)*

(Maestoso andante)

Key ___: _____

*This movement is found in its entirety in *Analytical Anthology of Music*, second edition, by Ralph Turek (McGraw-Hill, Inc., 1992).

4 Mozart: *The Magic Flute, K. 620* (Act 1, No. 8)

(Allegro)

schön!   La la ra,   la la   la la ra, la   la   la la ra.

Key ___: _____

B. Realize the following figured bass passages and identify the type of six-four chord in each. Provide a harmonic analysis.

1 Six-four chord: _____

2 Six-four chord: _____

Key __: __ __ __ __ __

Key __: __ __ __ __ __

3 Six-four chord: _____

4 Six-four chord: _____

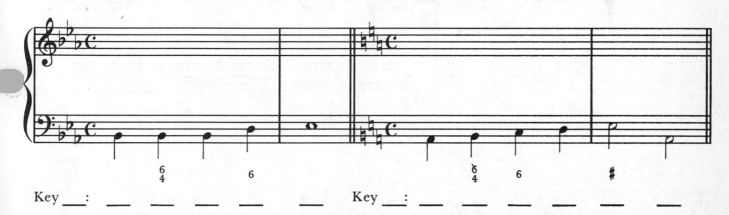

Key __: __ __ __ __ __

Key __: __ __ __ __ __

5 Six-four chord: _____

6 Six-four chord: _____

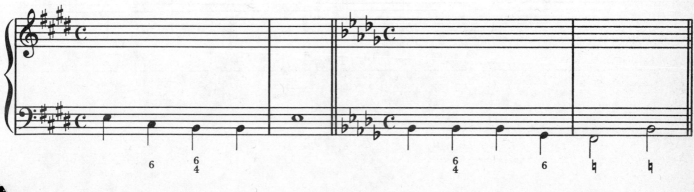

Key __: __ __ __ __ __

Key __: __ __ __ __ __

C. Add the three missing voices to the following passages, using a cadential, passing, or pedal six-four chord at the point indicated. Then provide a harmonic analysis. (Bass lines are unfigured.)

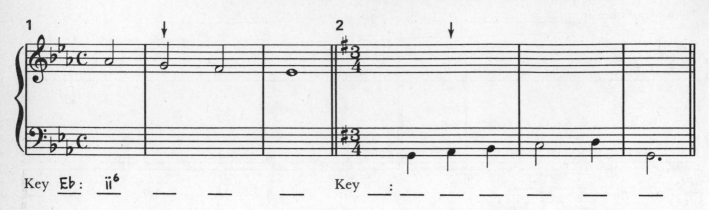

Key Eb: ii⁶ _ _ _ _   Key _ : _ _ _ _

Key d: i _ _ _ _ _   Key Gb: _ _ _ _ _

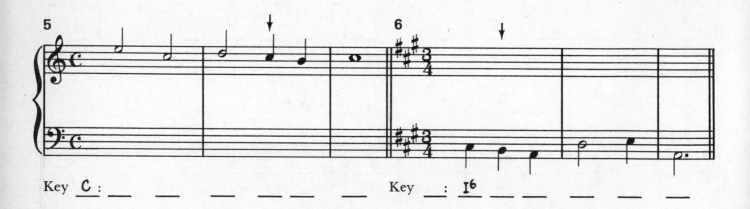

Key C: _ _ _ _ _   Key _ : I⁶ _ _ _ _

A. 1. Identify features of the voice leading not in keeping with the norms described in Unit Three. (Refer to the Voice-Leading Guide on page 219.) In each passage, a six-four chord has been used in an *atypical* way. Explain the problem.

   2. Retain the melody and rewrite the passage, eliminating the voice-leading errors. You may use different inversions or different harmonies as needed.

1 "Alle Menschen müssen sterben"

Rewrite:

2 "Herr, wie du willst, so schick's mit mir"

Rewrite:

NOTE: J. S. Bach's harmonizations of these chorales appear as Nos. 153 and 317 in the *371 Harmonized Chorales and 69 Chorale Melodies* edited by Albert Riemenschneider (G. Schirmer, 1941).

B. Complete the following in four voices and provide a harmonic analysis.
   Identify all six-four chords by type (cadential, passing, pedal, or arpeggiated).

1

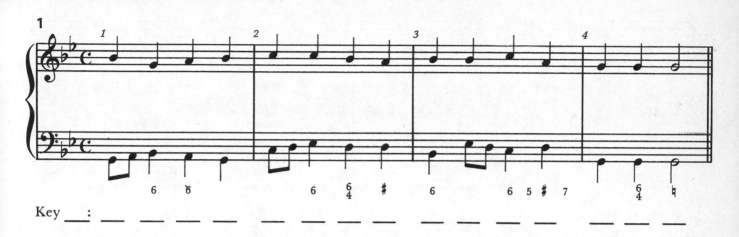

Key ___: _ _ _ _ _ _ _ _ _ _ _ _ _ _ _ _ _

2

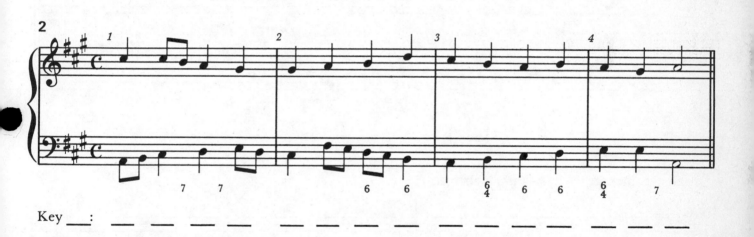

Key ___: _ _ _ _ _ _ _ _ _ _ _ _ _ _ _ _ _

3

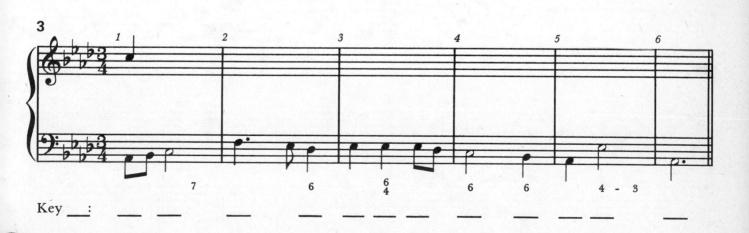

Key ___: _ _ _ _ _ _ _ _ _ _ _ _ _ _ _ _ _

C. Provide a harmonic analysis of the following chorale fragments. Disregard the chords enclosed in boxes. Circle and label all nonchord tones. Identify all six-four chords as cadential, passing, pedal, or arpeggiated. *Note:* In certain chorales, the key signature does not reflect the actual key.

J. S. Bach: "Jesu, Jesu, du bist mein"

Key ___ : _____

_____

J. S. Bach: "Was frag' ich nach der Welt"

Key ___ : _____

A: _____

Harmonize the following melodies, observing the principles of functional harmony that you have already learned. Write out the chords in root position on the blank staff beneath the melody. On the next blank staff, write the bass line formed by the chord roots. Next, use inversions and passing tones to create a smoother bass line. Finally, provide a four-part realization of your harmonization.

1

Chords:

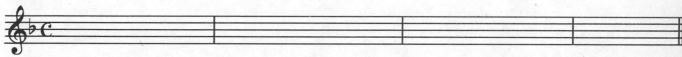

Bass line formed by chord roots:

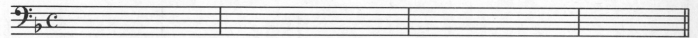

Bass line after inversions and passing tones:

Four-part realization:

2

Chords:

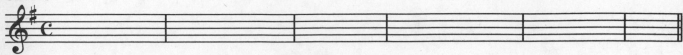

Bass line formed by chord roots:

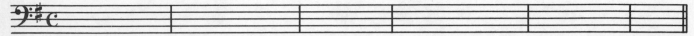

Bass line after inversions and passing tones:

Four-part realization:

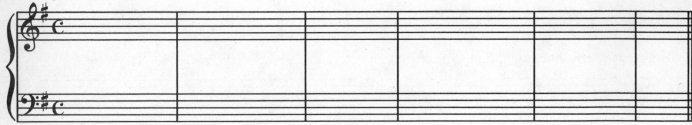

3

Chords:

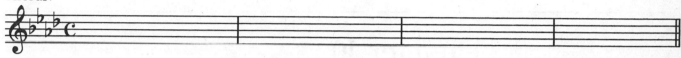

Bass line formed by chord roots:

Bass line after inversions and passing tones:

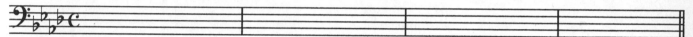

Four-part realization:

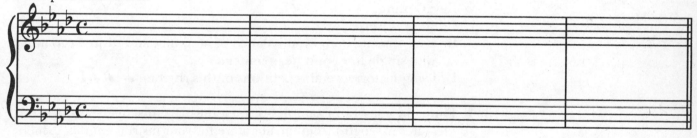

Melody

Chapter 10
Melody

PARTS ONE and TWO

A. Compose short melodies, as specified below.

1 $\frac{4}{4}$ meter; eight-measure length
   Key: A major
   Contour: arch
   Interval structure: prevailingly conjunct, with single high point near
      center of arch
   Unifying factor: several repetitions of this rhythm: ♩ ♫

2 $\frac{3}{4}$ meter; six-measure length
   Key: G minor
   Contour: inverted arch
   Interval structure: an even balance of conjunct and disjunct motion,
      with single low point near center
   Unifying factor: several repetitions of this rhythm: ♩. ♪♫

B. **1** Find and copy two examples of melodies (from sixteen to thirty-two
   measures in length) from the literature for your instrument that exhibit:

   a. homogeneous rhythmic patterns.
   b. diverse rhythmic patterns.

   2 Identify the most frequently used patterns in each melody. Identify
   the pitch basis and tonal center for each.

C. Answer the following questions concerning the melodies that appear
   below.

   1 General character:

   a. Name the scalar basis.
   b. Describe the contours formed by the bracketed segments.
   c. Identify the most prominent rhythmic pattern by circling its first
      appearance.

2 Tonal character. Show how the tonality is established through:

a. emphasis on the tonic and dominant scale degrees (use *T* and *D* to signify tonic and dominant pitches that are stressed through duration, metric placement, or register).

b. prominent outlining of the tonic, dominant, and subdominant triads (use brackets and Roman numerals).

c. resolution of tendency tones (draw an arrow from each prominent tendency tone to its resolution pitch).

Haydn: *String Quartet, Op. 9, No. 6, H. III:24* (III)

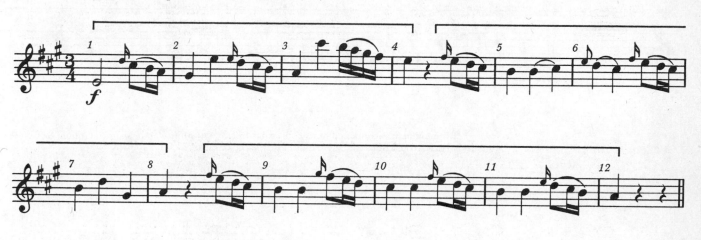

Kuhlau: *Sonatina, Op. 20, No. 2*

Schumann: *Album for the Young, Op. 68* (No. 8, "Wild Rider")*

*This movement is contained in its entirety in *Anthology for Musical Analysis,* fifth edition, by Charles Burkhart (Harcourt Brace College Publishers, 1994).

Beethoven: *Piano Sonata, Op. 22* (III)

PART THREE

A. For each of the melodic figures below, compose the specified passage.

1

a: a real sequence a major third above   **b:** a tonal sequence a minor third below

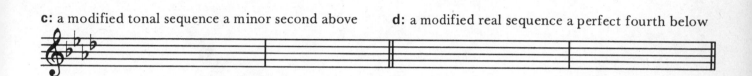

c: a modified tonal sequence a minor second above   **d:** a modified real sequence a perfect fourth below

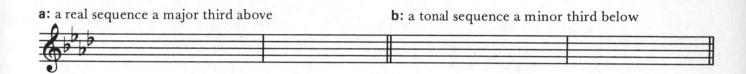

2

a: a real sequence a major third above   **b:** a tonal sequence a minor third below

c: a modified tonal sequence a minor second above   **d:** a modified real sequence a perfect fourth below

3

a: a real sequence a major third above   **b:** a tonal sequence a minor third below

c: a modified tonal sequence a minor second above   **d:** a modified real sequence a perfect fourth below

B. Compose sequences, as specified, to the following figures:

1   Tonal sequence a major second lower

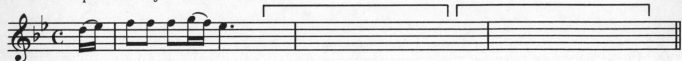

2   Real sequence a major third higher

3   Tonal sequence a diatonic third higher

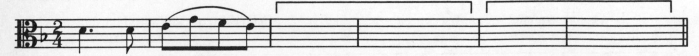

4   Real sequence a major third lower

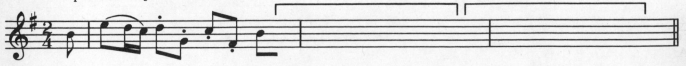

C. In the following sequential passages:

1. Bracket and label the first statement and each subsequent statement of the pattern.
2. Identify the sequence as real or tonal, or as modified real or tonal.
3. Indicate the level of transposition at each repetition.

NOTE: The key in which each passage begins is given. It may or may not change during the course of the sequence.

1 Mozart: *Minuet, K. 2*

g:

2 Corelli: *Violin Sonata, Op. 5, No. 9* (II)

A:

3 Beethoven: *Piano Sonata, Op. 10, No. 1* (I)

f:

4 Haydn: *Piano Sonata, H. XVI:19* (II)

A:

5 Couperin: *Suites de Pièces pour le Clavecin, 3ème Ordre* ("La Favorite")

c:

6 Schubert: *Piano Sonata, D. 960* (I)

c#:

7 J. S. Bach: *The Well-Tempered Clavier, Book I* (Prelude No. 17, *BWV 862*)

E♭:

Chapter 11
Large-Scale Melodic Relationships

A. Four melodies are given with melodic reductions shown beneath them. Using as a model the measure-for-measure account on page 282 of the text, explain why each note has been represented as it has been in the reduction. Feel free to offer an alternative analysis if you disagree with certain aspects of the reduction. Be sure to support your alternative analysis with solid arguments. The chords are indicated by letter name symbols. (Inversions are not indicated.)

1 Schumann: *Album for the Young, Op. 68* (No. 11, "Sicilienne")

2 Handel: *Suite in D Minor, HWV 448* (Chaconne)

3 Mozart: *String Quartet, K. 421* (IV)

4 Mozart: *Sonata for Violin and Piano, K. 296* (II)

B. In the following exercises, compose a melody around the given structural tones, maintaining their *approximate* positions. Add supporting and embellishing tones and incorporate a step progression. Strive for rhythmic variety but try to organize each melody around a rhythmic motive. As a first step, decide which structural tones are to act as melodic cadence points. This will determine the phrase structure of the melody.

1

2

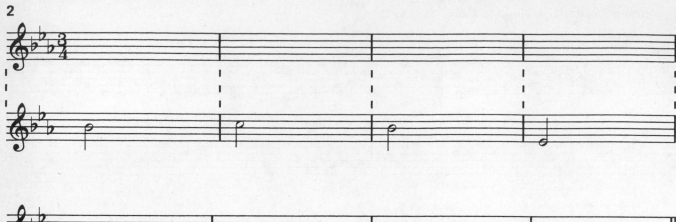

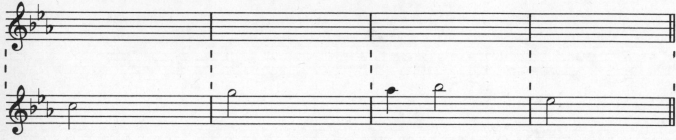

C. Use arrows to indicate the large-scale arpeggiations, and use brackets to show the step progressions contained in the following excerpts.

1 Mozart: *String Quartet, K. 421* (III)

2 Haydn: *Piano Sonata, XVI:29* (Menuetto)

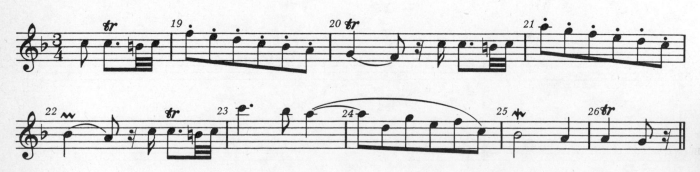

3 J. S. Bach: *English Suite No. 6, BWV 811* (Gavotte II)

4 Schubert: "Ungeduld," No. 17 (from *Die schöne Müllerin, D. 795)**

*This song is contained in its entirety in *Analytical Anthology of Music,* second edition, by Ralph Turek (McGraw-Hill, Inc., 1992).

5 Beethoven: *Piano Sonata, Op. 2, No. 1* (I)*

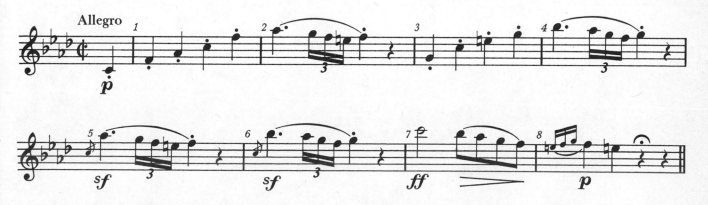

*This movement is contained in its entirety in *Anthology for Musical Analysis,* fifth edition, by Charles Burkhart (Harcourt Brace College Publishers, 1994).

6 Mozart: *Concerto for Clarinet and Orchestra, K. 622 (I)**

*This movement is contained in its entirety in *Analytical Anthology of Music,* second edition, by Ralph Turek (McGraw-Hill, Inc., 1992).

Chapter 12
Melodic Form

PART ONE

A. For each pair of phrases:

1. Identify their relationship, using the symbols a a, a a′, a b_{sim}, or a b_{contr}.
2. In a sentence or two, explain why you analyzed the relationship as you did.
3. Alter the second phrase so that it forms the requested relationship with the first phrase.

1

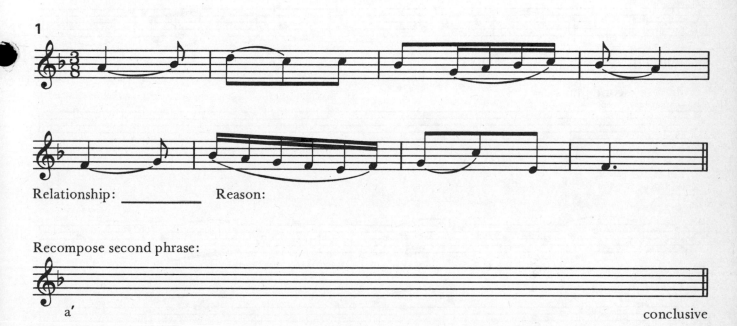

Relationship: _____   Reason:

Recompose second phrase:

a′   conclusive

2

Relationship: _____ Reason:

Recompose second phrase:

bcontr   conclusive

3

Relationship: _____ Reason:

Recompose second phrase:

a′   conclusive

4

Relationship: _____ Reason:

Recompose second phrase:

a′   conclusive

104

5

Relationship: _____ Reason:

Recompose second phrase:

b_{sim}   conclusive

B. Compose sixteen-measure melodies according to the following specifications.

1 First phrase: ascending contour; conjunct interval structure; conclusive cadence
  Second phrase: descending contour; disjunct interval structure; conclusive cadence
  Pitch basis: D major
  Meter: simple duple

2 First phrase: stationary contour; conjunct interval structure; inconclusive cadence
  Second phrase: archlike contour; conjunct interval structure; conclusive cadence
  Pitch basis: G minor
  Meter: compound duple

A. For each phrase given below, compose another (either the first or the second), so that the two phrases relate as specified.

Similar phrase forming a period

Contrasting phrase forming a period

Varied repetition not forming a period

4

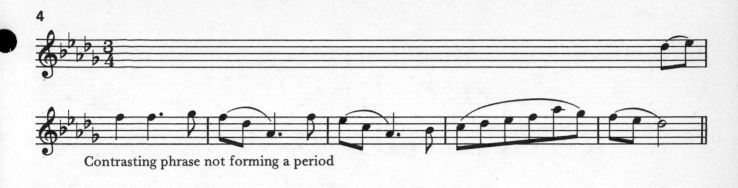

Contrasting phrase not forming a period

5

Varied repetition forming a period

B. For the following excerpts:

1. Identify each phrase and use letter names to indicate the phrase relationships.
2. Indicate whether or not the phrases in combination form a period and, if so, what kind.
3. Bracket all sequences and indicate the type.
4. Identify all step progressions and large-scale arpeggiations.
5. Provide a harmonic analysis.

1 Anonymous: *Notebook for Anna Magdelena Bach, BWV Anh. 115**

Key ___ : ___ ___ ___ ___ ___ ___ ___

2 Haydn: *Sonata H. XVI:37 (I)**

Allegro con brio

Key ___: ___

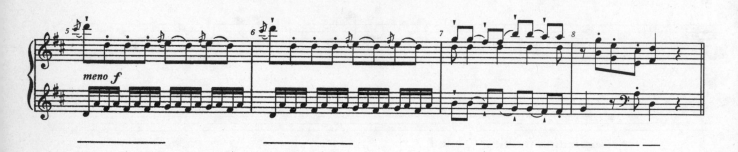

3 Mozart: *Eine Kleine Nachtmusik K. 525 (III)**

Trio
(Allegretto)

Key ___: ___

*These three movements are contained in their entirety in *Analytical Anthology of Music,* second edition, by Ralph Turek (McGraw-Hill, Inc., 1992).

C. Compose a varied repetition of each of the following phrases, ending
   with a cadential extension.

1

Varied repetition with cadential extension (beginning with last beat of m. 4)

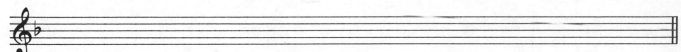

2

Varied repetition with cadential extension

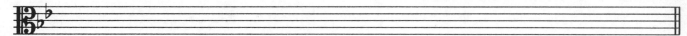

3

Varied repetition with cadential extension

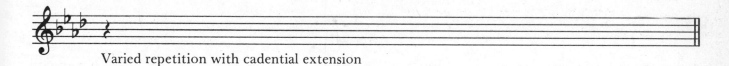

4

Varied repetition with cadential extension (beginning with last beat of m. 4)

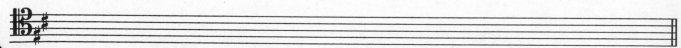

PART THREE

Provide a complete melodic analysis of the following excerpt, using the Outline for Melodic Analysis on text pages 307–308 and the subsequent analytical discussion as a guide.

Mozart: *Piano Concerto, K. 488* (I)*

*This movement appears in its entirety in *Anthology for Musical Analysis*, fifth edition, by Charles Burkhart (Harcourt Brace College Publishers, 1994).

Further Harmonic Resources

Chapter 13
*Diatonic Seventh Chords I: The Dominant
Seventh and Leading-Tone Seventh Chords*

PART ONE

A. Beneath each chord, indicate the key in which it functions as a V⁷. Place
an *X* beneath any chord that is *not* a dominant seventh type.

Key:

B. Beneath the given soprano pitch, construct in four voices a root-position dominant seventh chord in close or open structure, as specified. Do not omit any chord tones.

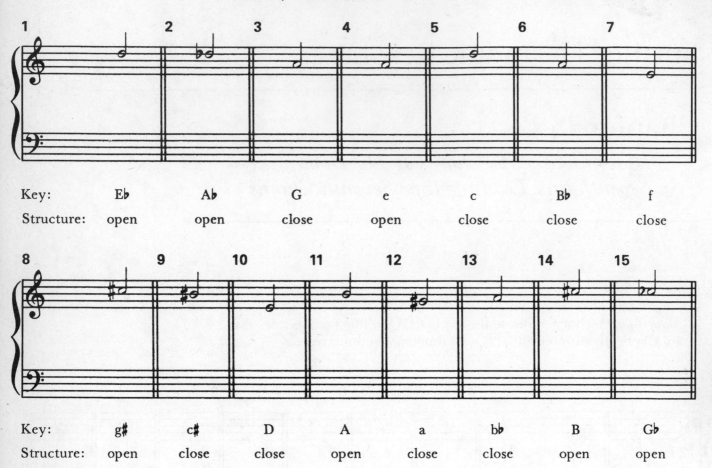

Key:	Eb	Ab	G	e	c	Bb	f
Structure:	open	open	close	open	close	close	close

Key:	g#	c#	D	A	a	bb	B	Gb
Structure:	open	close	close	open	close	close	open	open

C. Resolve each of the following figured bass patterns. Then provide harmonic analysis.

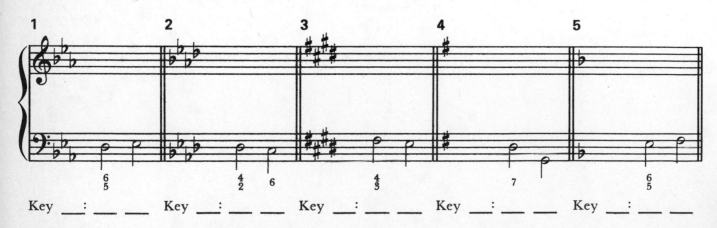

Key ___ : ___ ___   Key ___ : ___ ___   Key ___ : ___ ___   Key ___ : ___ ___   Key ___ : ___ ___

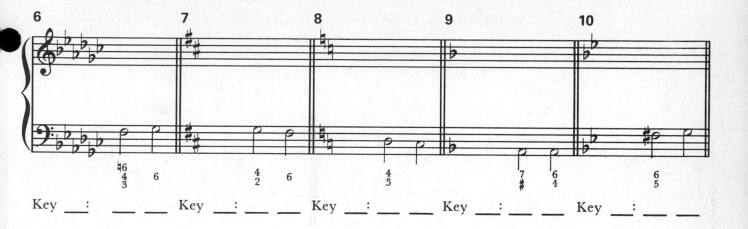

Key ___:___ ___   Key ___:___ ___   Key ___:___ ___   Key ___:___ ___   Key ___:___ ___

D. Observing principles of correct voice leading, add three voices above the given bass lines. At the point indicated, construct a V⁷ in which the seventh resembles the specified nonchord tone. Provide harmonic analysis of each passage. (Be sure to indicate the key.)

Key ___:___ ___ ___   Key ___:___ ___   Key ___:___ ___

Key ___:___ ___ ___   Key ___:___ ___ ___

A. Identify by Roman numeral and superscript the following dominant seventh and leading-tone seventh chords.

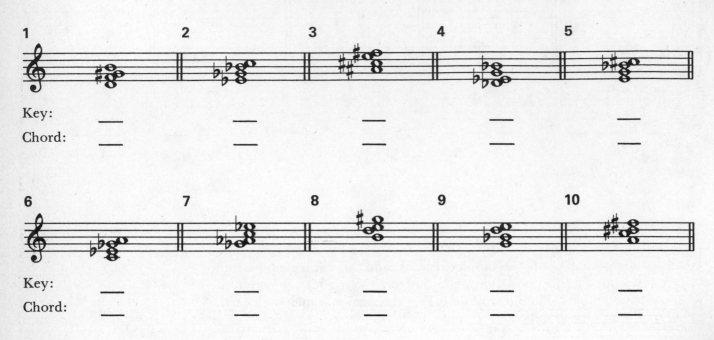

Key: ___   ___   ___   ___   ___

Chord: ___   ___   ___   ___   ___

Key: ___   ___   ___   ___   ___

Chord: ___   ___   ___   ___   ___

B. Write the requested chord in the specified inversion.

G: V_3^4 eb: vii^{o6}_5 Ab: $vii^{\emptyset 4}_2$ D: V_2^4 B: $vii^{\emptyset 6}_5$

f: V_5^6 a: V_3^4 A: $vii^{\emptyset 4}_2$ E: V_5^6 c#: vii^{o4}_3

C. Resolve the following leading-tone seventh chords appropriately. Then
   provide analysis symbols.

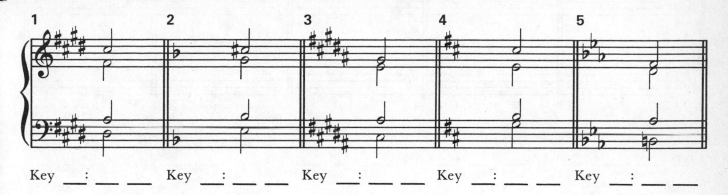

Key __:__ __ __   Key __:__ __ __   Key __:__ __ __   Key __:__ __ __   Key __:__ __ __

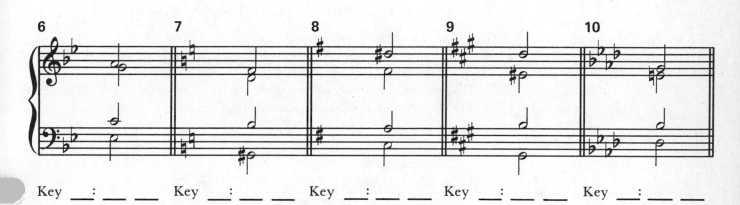

Key __:__ __ __   Key __:__ __ __   Key __:__ __ __   Key __:__ __ __   Key __:__ __ __

D. Part-write the following two-chord successions and provide a Roman
   numeral analysis. Then practice playing each at the keyboard.

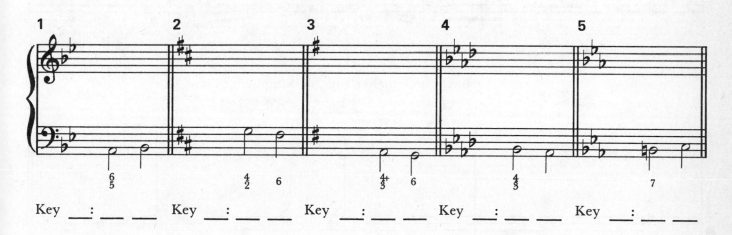

Key __:__ __   Key __:__ __   Key __:__ __   Key __:__ __   Key __:__ __

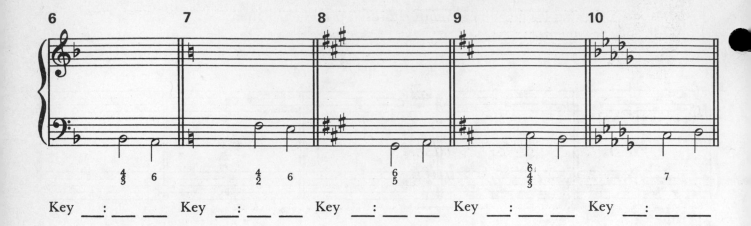

Key ___:___ ___ Key ___:___ ___ Key ___:___ ___ Key ___:___ ___ Key ___:___ ___

E. Following is an excerpt from a chorale harmonization by J. S. Bach.

   1 Circle and label all nonchord tones.
   2 Locate and identify with appropriate chord symbols three dominant seventh chords.
   3 Discuss the resolution of the tendency tones in each of these chords.
   4 Locate a suspension and discuss its resolution.

J. S. Bach: "Nun danket alle Gott"

F. Part-write and analyze the following figured bass line.

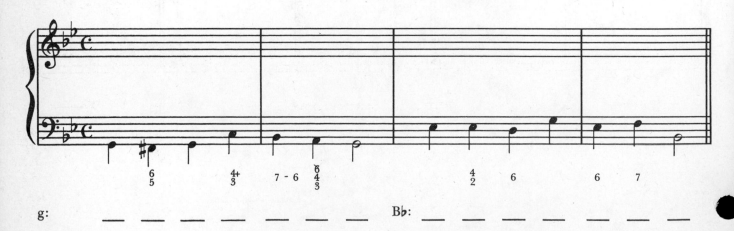

g: ___ ___ ___ ___ ___   Bb: ___ ___ ___ ___ ___

Chapter 14
Diatonic Seventh Chords II:
Nondominant Seventh Chords

PART ONE

A. Identify the type of seventh chord (Mm[7], mm[7], etc.) in each measure.

B. Spell the specified seventh chord in root position, regarding the given pitch as the root, third, fifth, or seventh, as indicated. Do not alter the given pitch.

Examples:

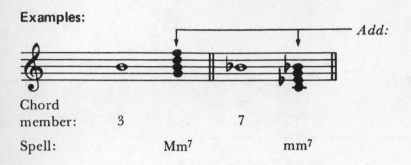

Chord member:	3		7
Spell:	Mm⁷		mm⁷

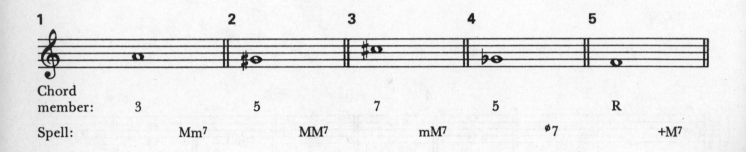

Chord member:	3	5	7	5	R
Spell:	Mm⁷	MM⁷	mM⁷	∅7	+M⁷

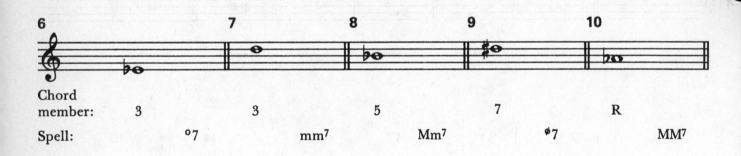

Chord member:	3	3	5	7	R
Spell:	°7	mm⁷	Mm⁷	∅7	MM⁷

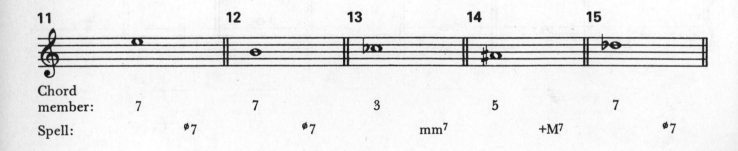

Chord member:	7	7	3	5	7
Spell:	∅7	∅7	mm⁷	+M⁷	∅7

C. Add the key signature and write the requested seventh chord in four voices,
using the specified structure and placing the seventh in the specified voice.

Example:

S = soprano
A = alto
T = tenor
B – bass

d: ii$^{\emptyset 7}$
             open
           7th in T

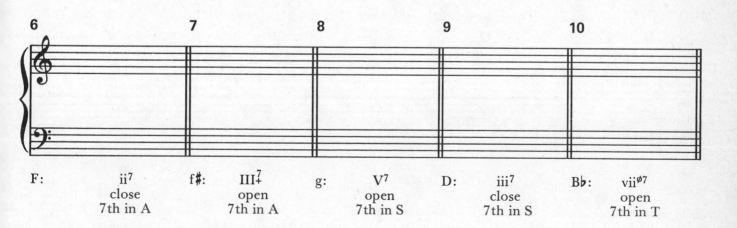

1		2		3		4		5	
a:	VI^7	c♯:	vii^{o7}	G♭:	iii^7	A♭:	IV^7	E:	vii$^{\emptyset 7}$
	close		open		open		close		open
	7th in T		7th in A		7th in A		7th in T		7th in S

6		7		8		9		10	
F:	ii^7	f♯:	III^7	g:	V^7	D:	iii^7	B♭:	vii$^{\emptyset 7}$
	close		open		open		close		open
	7th in A		7th in A		7th in S		7th in S		7th in T

119

D. In each line below, consider the given tone as the root, third, fifth, or seventh of a seventh chord, as specified. Construct the root-position chord as it would appear in the keys listed. Then, provide the Roman numeral symbol for each.

Example:

Pitch is third

Db: V^7 F: iii^7 bb: vii^{o7} c: VI^7 g: $ii^{ø7}$

1 Pitch is fifth

Db: ___   Eb: ___   F: ___   g: ___   Ab: ___

2 Pitch is third

D: ___   E: ___   B: ___   G: ___   e: ___

3 Pitch is seventh

B: ___   a: ___   g#: ___   D: ___   G: ___

4 Pitch is fifth

Eb: ___   g: ___   bb: ___   C: ___   c: ___

5 Pitch is third

g: ___   D: ___   A: ___   Bb: ___   F: ___

E. Using Illustrations 14.2, 14.3, and 14.5 on pages 351–352 of the text as a reference, notate the following.

1 The three mm^7 chords in E major

2 The two MM^7 chords in B minor

3 The two pre-dominant seventh chords in F♯ major

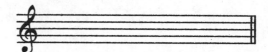

4 Two mm^7 chords in D minor

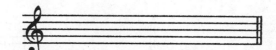

5 The two MM^7 chords in A♭ major

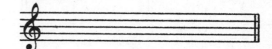

6 The three mm^7 chords in G major

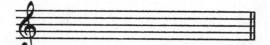

7 The two pre-dominant seventh chords in A minor

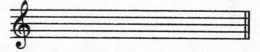

8 Two mm^7 chords in C♯ minor

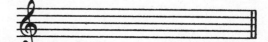

9 The two MM^7 chords in D major

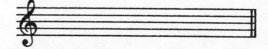

10 The three mm^7 chords in B♭ major

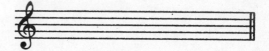

PART TWO

A. Write the indicated seventh chords in the four-voice structure specified.

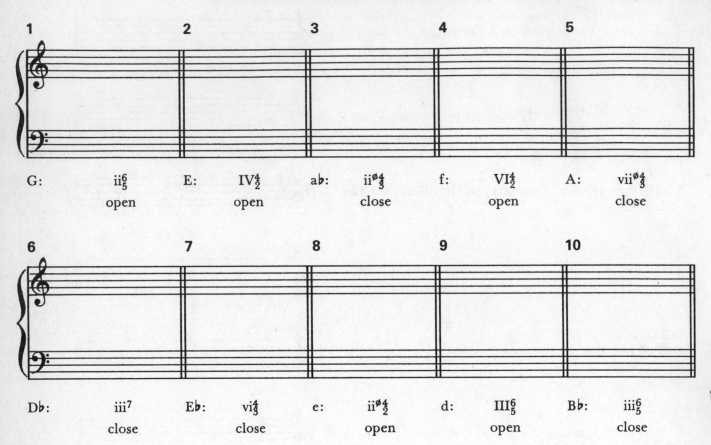

1	2	3	4	5
G: ii$^6_5$	E: IV$^4_2$	a♭: ii$^{ø4}_3$	f: VI$^4_2$	A: vii$^{ø4}_3$
open	open	close	open	close

6	7	8	9	10
D♭: iii^7	E♭: vi$^4_3$	e: ii$^{ø4}_2$	d: III$^6_5$	B♭: iii$^6_5$
close	close	open	open	close

B. Add three voices above the following figured bass line.

6   7 - 6   7 - 6   4 - 3   7 - 6   7 - 6   4 - 3

122

C. Provide harmonic analysis of the following excerpts. Notate the seventh chords in root position on the staff below. Above each seventh chord, indicate the nature of the seventh (suspension, passing tone, and so on), and draw an arrow to its note of resolution. The first few beats have been completed for you.

1 Grieg: *Holberg Suite* (Musette)

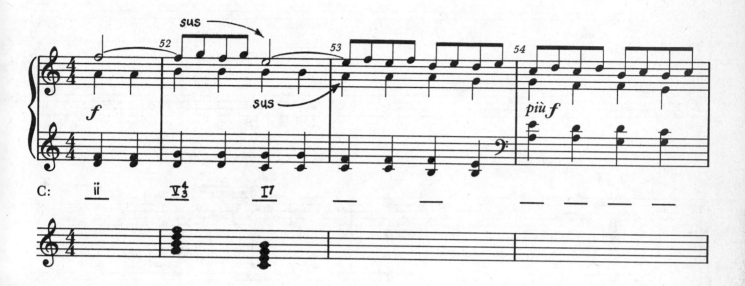

G:

*This prelude is contained in its entirety in *Analytical Anthology of Music*, second edition, by Ralph Turek (McGraw-Hill, Inc., 1992).

D. Add the root-position seventh chord whose root lies a fifth above the given chord's root. Then provide harmonic analysis. Observe principles of correct voice leading. Be particularly careful to place the seventh in the voice that permits its stepwise downward resolution. Then practice playing each succession at the keyboard.

E. Add the key signature and part-write the following two-chord successions for four voices.

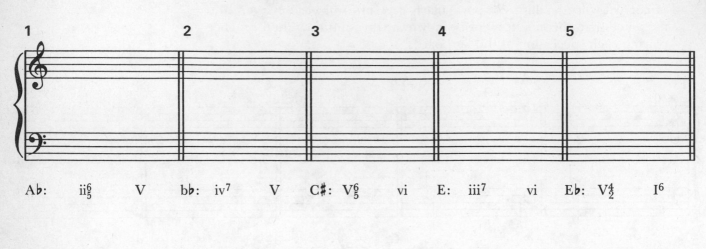

1   A♭:   ii$^6_5$ V   2   b♭:   iv^7 V   3   C♯:   V$^6_5$ vi   4   E: iii^7 vi   5   E♭:   V$^4_2$ I^6

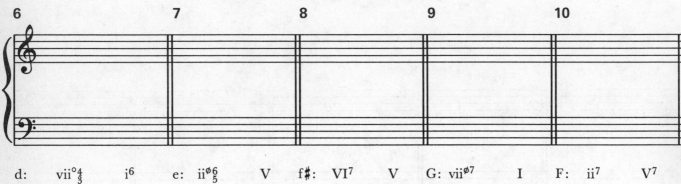

6   d: vii°$^4_3$ i^6 7   e: ii$^{ø6}_5$ V   8   f♯:   VI^7 V   9   G: vii^{ø7} I   10   F: ii^7 V^7

A. Successions of seventh chords are indicated by the following figured bass lines. Part-write the bass lines, using incomplete seventh chords only where necessary. Then provide harmonic analysis.

1

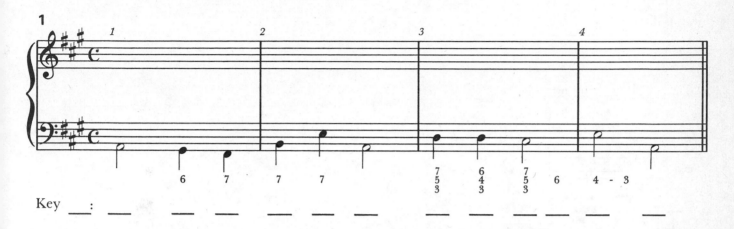

Key ___ : __ __ __ __ __ __ __ __ __ __

2

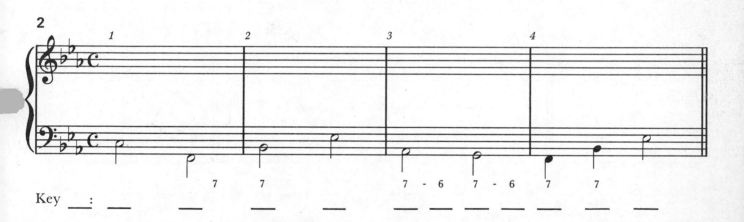

Key ___ : __ __ __ __ __ __ __ __ __

3

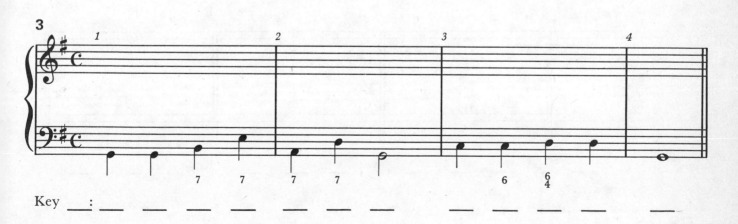

Key ___ : __ __ __ __ __ __ __ __ __ __

B. Following are alternative minor-key seventh chords—either the IV⁷ (an alternative to the iv⁷) or the vi°⁷ (an alternative to the VI⁷). Determine the key and place the appropriate chord symbol beneath each. Add the key signature and resolve the chord in such a way that the raised sixth scale degree moves upward and the chord seventh resolves downward.

Example:

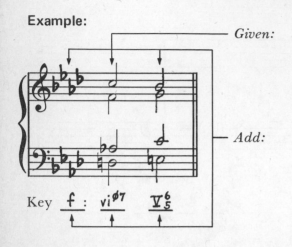

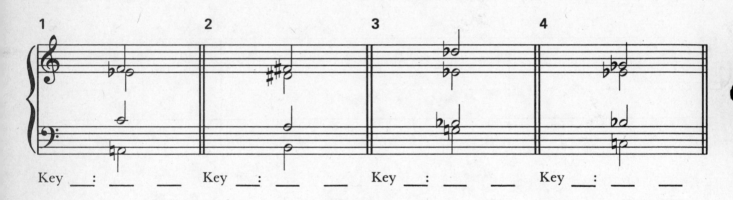

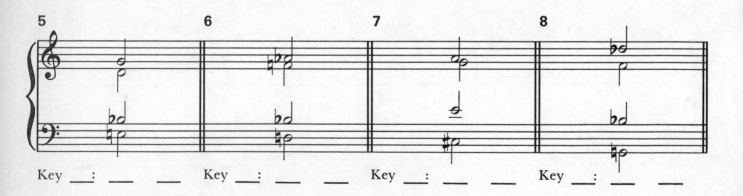

C. Part-write the following figured bass lines in four voices. Resolve all sevenths downward by step, even if such a resolution requires a less common doubling. Then provide harmonic analysis.

Key ___ : ___ ___ ___ ___ ___ ___ ___ ___

Key ___ : ___ ___ ___ ___ ___ ___ ___

Chapter 15
Secondary Function

PART ONE

A. Give the Roman numeral symbol (with appropriate superscripts) that represents each chord's function in the indicated keys.

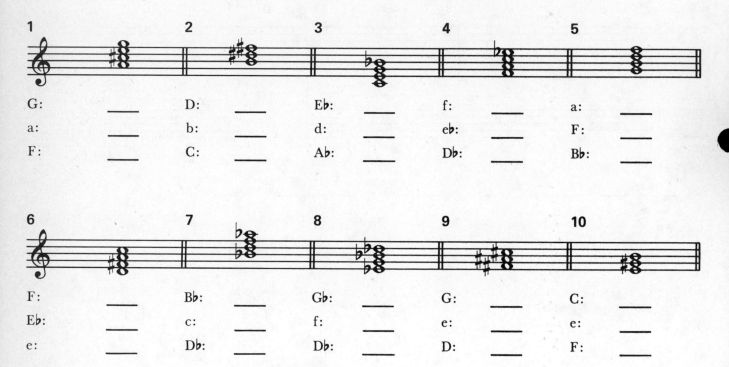

1		2		3		4		5	
G:	___	D:	___	Eb:	___	f:	___	a:	___
a:	___	b:	___	d:	___	eb:	___	F:	___
F:	___	C:	___	Ab:	___	Db:	___	Bb:	___

6		7		8		9		10	
F:	___	Bb:	___	Gb:	___	G:	___	C:	___
Eb:	___	c:	___	f:	___	e:	___	e:	___
e:	___	Db:	___	Db:	___	D:	___	F:	___

B. In the following measures, add the key signature and then show the
figured bass that would properly indicate the specified chord and inversion. Be sure to include necessary accidentals in the figured bass symbol.

Example:

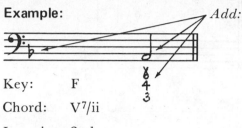

Key: F
Chord: V⁷/ii
Inversion: 2nd

1	2	3	4	5

	1	2	3	4	5
Key:	D♭	e♭	B♭	B	E
Chord:	V/iii	V⁷/iv	V⁷/vi	V/ii	V/V
Inversion:	root	root	2nd	1st	1st

6	7	8	9	10

	6	7	8	9	10
Key:	d	A	A♭	b♭	g
Chord:	V⁷/VI	V⁷/iii	V/vi	V⁷/VI	V/V
Inversion:	3rd	2nd	1st	1st	root

C. Considering the key signature and the given harmonies, provide the
most probable harmonic analysis.

Key __ : __ __ __ __   Key __ : __ __ __ __ __   Key __ : __ __ __ __ __

Key ___ : ___ ___ ___ ___ ___   Key ___ : ___ ___ ___ ___ ___   Key ___ : ___ ___ ___ ___ ___

PART TWO

A. In this exercise, the first chord given is the tonic. Between it and the following chord, insert the specified type of secondary function. Then complete the harmonic analysis. Be sure to add all sharps or flats, since key signatures are not supplied.

Example:

Given this: *Complete like this:*

Ab: I   vii°⁷/ ___ ___   Ab: I   vii°⁷/ ii   ii

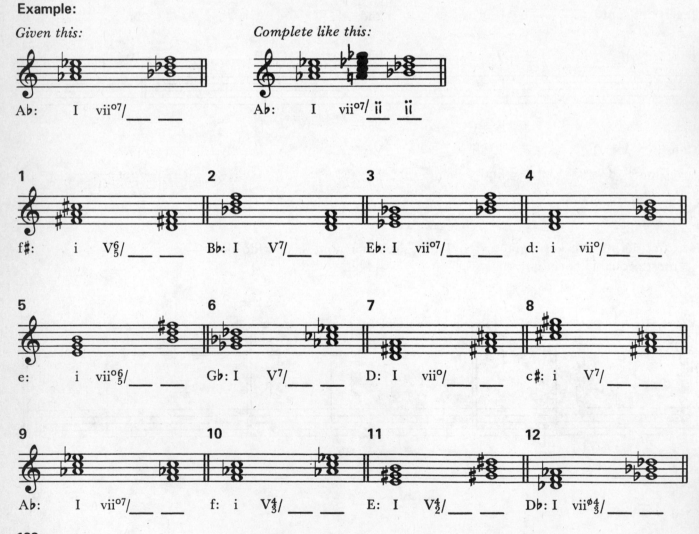

B. Show the Roman numeral that represents each chord's function in the indicated keys.

Example:

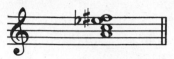

c: vii°$^6_5$/$\underline{V}$ (or vii°$^6_5$/v)
E♭: vii°$^6_5$/iii
F: vii°$^6_5$/ii

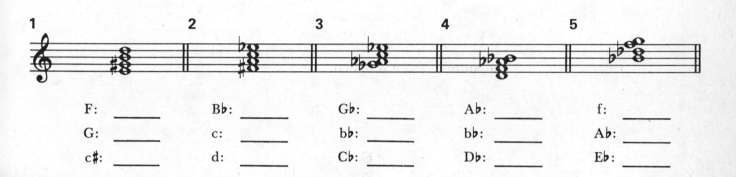

1	2	3	4	5
F: _____	B♭: _____	G♭: _____	A♭: _____	f: _____
G: _____	c: _____	b♭: _____	b♭: _____	A♭: _____
c♯: _____	d: _____	C♭: _____	D♭: _____	E♭: _____

6	7	8	9	10
B: _____	d♯: _____	e♭: _____	A: _____	E♭: _____
c♯: _____	A: _____	G♭: _____	E: _____	F: _____
A: _____	E: _____	a♭: _____	F♯: _____	C: _____

C. On the blank staff beneath the following excerpt from Beethoven's *Symphony No. 1*, write the harmonies in their simplest form. Then provide harmonic analysis. The passage begins and ends in C and all instruments are nontransposing (that is, they sound as written). Draw an arrow from each chromatic tone to its note of resolution. Circle each chord's seventh and draw an arrow pointing to its note of resolution. (If these notes are doubled, you need show only one case.) Having done this, what generalizations can you make concerning these tendency tones?

Beethoven: *Symphony No. 1, Op. 21* (I)

D. For the following excerpt:

1 Analyze the phrase-period structure in the manner learned in Chapter Twelve. Do the phrases form a period? If so, what kind?

2 Provide harmonic analysis of mm. 81–92. Identify any six-four chords as cadential, passing, pedal, or arpeggiated. *Note:* The harmonic rhythm is the quarter note. However, some nonchord tones do occur on the downbeat, in which case the true chords can be found at the point of resolution. Also, note that mm. 88–91 contain a pedal point in the 'cello part. This note sometimes is part of the harmony and sometimes is *not* part of the harmony.

3 If so instructed, continue harmonic analysis to the end of the excerpt. However, be aware that many nonchord tones are present in mm. 92–96.

Haydn: *String Quartet Op. 76, No. 3* (II)*

*This movement appears in its entirety in *Analytical Anthology of Music*, second edition, by Ralph Turek (McGraw-Hill, Inc., 1992).

PART THREE

A. Complete the following in four voices as indicated. Then, practice playing each exercise at the keyboard. In certain exercises, it *may* be necessary to use less common doublings in order to resolve the altered tones properly.

B. Analyze the harmonic implications in the following two-voice passages. The given notes constitute the root, third, or fifth of a triad, or perhaps the seventh of a seventh chord. Use your understanding of functional harmony and inversion along with your ear to determine the most appropriate harmonies. Be alert to the possibility of secondary functions. After adding Roman numerals, part-write the inner voices.

Key _____: ___ __ __ __ __ __ __ __ __ __ __

Key _____: ___ __ __ __ __ __ __ __ __

C. Using the steps outlined in this chapter, provide harmonizations for the following melodies, and incorporate secondary function where appropriate. Place chord symbols beneath the melody notes.

1

2

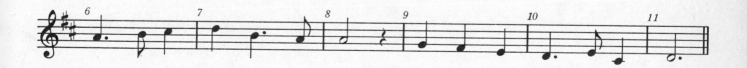

D. Realize the following figured bass line and provide a harmonic analysis.

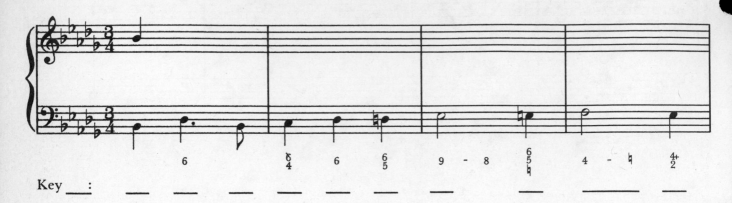

Key ___ : ___ ___ ___ ___ ___ ___ ___ ___

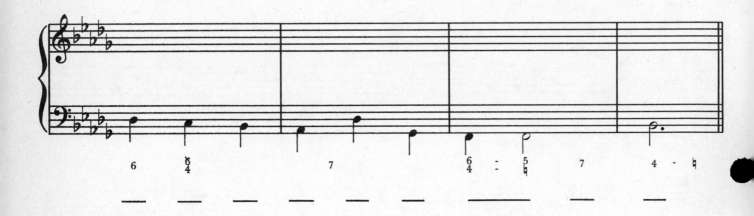

___ ___ ___ ___ ___ ___ ___

E. Provide a harmonic analysis of the following passage. Then describe the phrase structure. Is this a single, eight-measure phrase or two shorter phrases? If two shorter phrases, where does each begin and end? Do they form a period?

Mozart: *String Quartet K. 458* (Menuetto)

(Moderato)

Key ___ : _____

Chapter 16
Modulation to Closely Related Keys

PART ONE

A. In the following exercise, list the keys closely related to each given original key. Then, indicate which one of these keys would be suggested by the consistent appearance of the indicated accidentals. (Assume these accidentals to be the only ones that appear).

Example:

Original key	Closely related keys	Accidentals	New key implied
F	d, Bb, g, C, a	B, C#	d
1 Db		G, E	
2 e		D, F, G#	
3 Bb		F#	
4 c#		B	
5 d		C, Eb	
6 E		D	
7 B		E#	
8 Gb		C, D	
9 b		E#, G#, A	
10 Ab		Gb	

B. Notate the triads with a pre-dominant function in the new key that are available as common chords in the following modulations. If none are available, indicate *NA* next to the staff.

Example:

From A♭ to E♭:

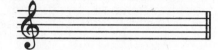

1 From g to B♭:

2 From D to A:

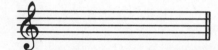

3 From F to B♭:

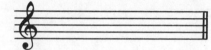

4 From E♭ to g:

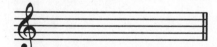

5 From B to g♯:

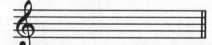

6 From c to A♭:

7 From e to D:

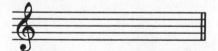

8 From D♭ to f:

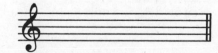

9 From F♯ to B:

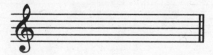

10 From f♯ to c♯:

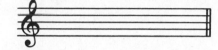

C. On a separate sheet of manuscript paper, realize the following bass lines and provide Roman numeral analysis, including the dual harmonic function of the pivot chord.

D. Treating the last chord given as a pre-dominant in the new key, complete the modulation to a closely related key. Once you have effected the modulation, continue with a suitable harmonic progression that confirms the new key, closing with an authentic cadence. The entire passage should be four measures long. Then provide a harmonic analysis.

2

3

4

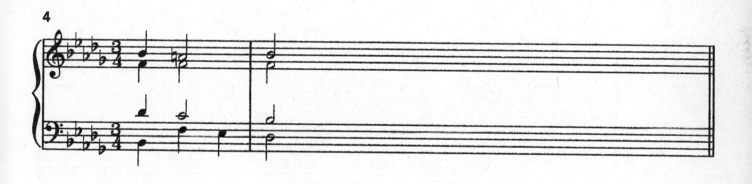

5

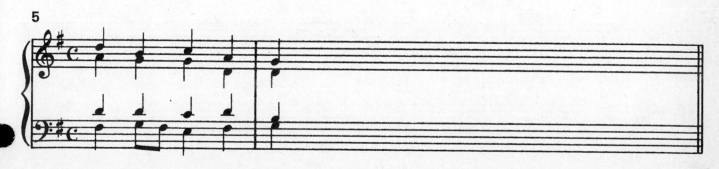

PARTS TWO and THREE

A. Complete the following four-part passages, employing chromatic modulations to the specified keys. The completed passage should comprise four measures. Your modulation should occur early enough to establish the new key in a convincing manner. Provide complete harmonic analysis.

1

to F

2

to e

3

to c#

4

to c

146

B. Harmonize the following melodies, including at least one modulation in each.

1. Write the Roman numerals representing your chosen root-position chords beneath the appropriate melody notes.
2. On the first blank staff, notate the root of each chord.
3. Use inversions and passing tones to create a more stepwise bass motion. Notate the figured bass line that represents this refinement on the second blank staff.
4. Identify the modulation as a pivot chord or chromatic type.

1 Schumann: "Nord oder Sud" (from *Songs for Mixed Choir, Op. 59*)

2 J. S. Bach: "Vergiss mein nicht"

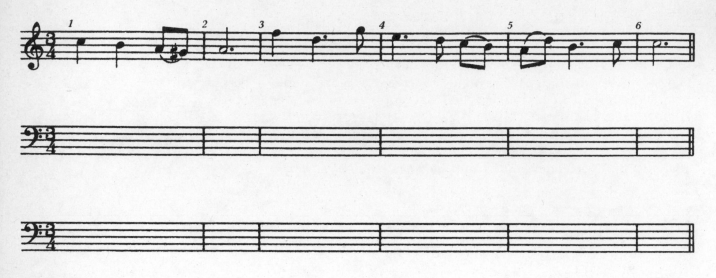

C. The following excerpt contains a number of *very short* modulations.* Provide harmonic analysis and identify each modulation as a pivot chord or chromatic type. If the modulation is by pivot chord, indicate the dual harmonic function of the pivot.

NOTE: In many cases, the first eighth note of the measure can be regarded as a pedal point or as a passing tone.

J. S. Bach: *Suite IV for Unaccompanied 'Cello, BWV 1010* (Prelude)

*It is equally appropriate to regard some of these modulations as tonicizations.

D. Provide a complete harmonic analysis and supply the requested additional information concerning the excerpt that follows.

1 The modulation occurs in m. _____ and is a _____ (pivot chord or chromatic type).

2 Escape tones can be found in m. _____ and m. _____.

3 An ANT is found in m. _____.

4 A 4-3 SUS with an ornamented resolution can be found in m. _____.

5 Describe the phrase-period structure. Be sure to identify the type of period, if one is formed.

J. S. Bach: *French Suite No. 6, BWV 817* (Sarabande)*

Key ___ :

*The complete movement, along with the minuet that follows, is contained in *Analytical Anthology of Music*, second edition, by Ralph Turek (McGraw-Hill, Inc. 1992).

E. Provide a complete harmonic analysis and supply the requested additional information concerning the excerpt that follows.

1 The excerpt begins in the key of _____ and ends in the key of _____.

2 The modulation occurs in m. _____ and is a _____ (pivot chord or chromatic type).

3 The second-inversion triad found in m. _____ is a _____ (cadential, passing, pedal, or arpeggiated) six-four chord.

4 What term best describes the piano's activity at mm. 32–33? _____ _____

Schubert: "Pause" (from *Die schöne Müllerin, D. 795*)*

*The complete song is contained in *Analytical Anthology of Music*, second edition, by Ralph Turek (McGraw-Hill, Inc. 1992).

151

Musical Form

Chapter 17
Form and Dramatic Shape in Music

A. Answer the questions concerning the two-part work that follows.

1 In what ways is the melody of the second half related to that of the first half?

2 Name a *non*melodic feature of the first half that is continued in the second half.

3 Compare the two halves from the standpoint of harmonic rhythm.

4 Provide a melodic reduction of the piece. Then explain the general difference in the structural melody in the two halves.

5 Which of these elements—melody, register, cadences, rhythm, texture, harmonic rhythm, articulation, dynamics, tempo—play the most important role in distinguishing the two sections? Which play *no* role?

NOTE: Disregard for now the role of tonality.

Brahms: *Waltz, Op. 39, No. 3*

B. Answer the questions concerning the two-part work that follows.

1 Describe the melodic similarities and differences in the two halves.
2 What is the most significant harmonic difference between the two halves?
3 Make a list—in order of importance—of the elements that you feel contribute most to the differences in the two sections.
4 Make a list of elements that you feel are essentially unchanged between the first and second sections.

Schubert: *Valse sentimentale, Op. 50, No. 10*

C. Analyze this movement, using as a model the analysis provided in the text
   on pages 443–444. Also, provide a complete harmonic analysis. As part
   of this analysis, identify all second-inversion triads by type (cadential,
   passing, pedal, or arpeggiated).

Haydn: *Piano Sonata, H. XVI:5* (Menuet)

Key ___ : ___ ___ ___ ___ ___

___ ___ ___ ___ ___ ___

___ ___ ___ ___ ___ ___ ___

Chapter 18
The Binary Principle

A. For the following work:

1 Provide a formal diagram that shows sections (upper-case letters), phrase structure (lower-case letters) and tonal plan.
2 Locate and identify each important cadence. Indicate which of these are the stronger and which are the weaker and explain why this is so.
3 Identify any modulations as pivot chord or chromatic types.

Anonymous (Anna Magdalena Bach's Notebook): *Minuet, BWV Anh. 118*

B. For the following work:

1. Provide a formal diagram that shows sections (upper-case letters), phrase structure (lower-case letters) and tonal plan.
2. Locate each important cadence. Indicate which of these are the stronger and which are the weaker and explain why this is so.
3. Identify any modulations as pivot chord or chromatic types.
4. Identify the two secondary functions that occur in the second part of the work.
5. Identify the types of six-four chord that occur in m. 3, m. 6, and m. 21. The first violin grace notes in mm. 3 and 6 are performed as follows:

Haydn: *String Quartet, Op. 17, No. 6, H. III:30* (Minuet)

C. For the following work:

1 Formal Structure: Provide a formal diagram of the movement similar to the diagram on page 451 of the text.

2 Melodic/Rhythmic Structure: Provide a melodic reduction of the right-hand part for the first and last eight measures.

3 Harmonic/Tonal Structure:

a Although mm. 5–6 and mm. 13–14 appear to be almost identical, they should probably be analyzed in different ways. Explain why and provide an appropriate analysis at each point.

b In the second half of this movement, examples of both modulation and tonicization occur before the original tonality returns. Identify each of these. When a tonicization occurs within a passage that is *not* in the principal tonality (i.e., one that has already modulated), symbolize the secondary function in relation to the *current* tonality.

c Which of the harmonic/tonal plans outlined on page 450 of the text does this movement most closely resemble and why?

d Provide harmonic analysis of mm. 1–16.

J. S. Bach: *French Suite No. 3, BWV 814* (Minuet)

Chapter 19
Rounded Binary and Ternary Forms

Answer the questions preceding each of the musical excerpts.

1 Formal Structure: Provide a diagram of the form, including principal sections (use capital letters) and phrases within (use lower-case letters). Follow the method given in the text (as on page 463).

   a Overall form:

   b Sections:

   c Phrases:

   d Cadences:

   e Tonality:

2 Melodic/Rhythmic Structure:

   a Provide a melodic reduction of mm. 1–8. Then identify any step progressions or large-scale arpeggiations that are present.

   b By what means does Mozart vary the phrase lengths in this movement? Give specific examples.

   c Identify one or two melodic features that are found in *all* sections of this movement.

3 Texture/Articulation/Dynamics: Do articulation and dynamics play any role in defining the form of this movement? Explain.

4 Harmonic/Tonal Structure: Give the Roman numeral symbol that represents the function of the following chords:

a m. 4, beat 3: _____

b m. 5, beat 3: _____

c m. 26, beat 3: _____

d m. 27, beat 1: _____

Mozart: *String Quartet, K. 458* (Menuetto)

1 This work is best analyzed as a ternary form. Provide a diagram that includes the principal sections (use capital letters) and the phrases within (use lower-case letters). Follow the method given in the text (as on page 467).

2 Which of the characteristics often found in ternary forms (see text page 464) are present in this piece?

3 In what ways is the middle section both similar to and different from the outer sections?

4 Show the tonal plan of the piece.

Schumann: *Album for the Young, Op. 68* (No. 3, "Humming Song")

1 Formal Structure:

   a List the features in this theme that support an analysis as rounded binary. Then list the features that support analysis as ternary. Which analysis do you prefer? Why?

   b Provide a complete diagram of the form, following the method given on text page 467.

2 Melodic/Rhythmic Structure: Discuss the sequential aspects of mm. 17–23.

3 Harmonic/Tonal Structure:

   a Illustrate the tonal plan of this theme.

   b Provide harmonic analysis of mm. 17–26.

4 Texture: Discuss the role of textural contrast in defining the sections of this theme.

Beethoven: *Piano Sonata, Op. 26* (I)

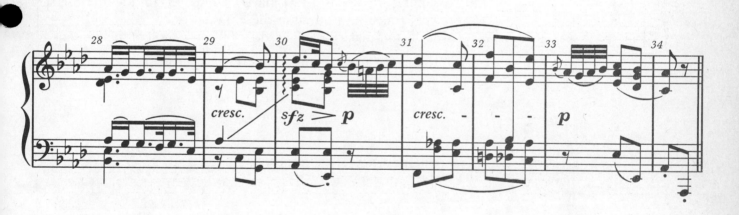

1 Formal Structure:

    a Identify the form as binary, rounded binary, or ternary and give your reasons.

    b Are the sections of this movement characterized more by similarity or by contrast? What are the most important factors contributing to this?

    c Which elements are most instrumental in creating the form?

2 Melodic/Rhythmic Structure:

    a Identify in the melodic line two separate sequences and describe them using appropriate terminology as discussed in Chapter Ten.

    b Locate one point at which sequences are present simultaneously in *all* the voices.

    c Disregarding the octave leaps, would you describe the bass line as primarily conjunct or disjunct?

3 Harmonic/Tonal Structure:

    a Name the principal key of the movement. At what point does the music clearly and finally return to this key?

    b To what key does the music modulate by m. 6? Does it remain there or does it immediately move elsewhere?

    c Identify the most prominent cadence aside from those at the double bars. Name the key and cadence type. At what point does the music move to this key? What creates the cadential effect at this point?

    d Assuming the key to be D major at mm. 15–16, identify the secondary functions present in these measures.

    e What factors make the final cadence the strongest of the movement?

4 Texture: Describe the texture, using the terms *homophonic* or *polyphonic*.

J. S. Bach: *Suite No. 3 for Orchestra, BWV 1068* (Air)